The Bible for the Curious

A Brief Encounter

The Bible for the Curious

A Brief Encounter

Philip R. Davies

SHEFFIELD UK   BRISTOL CT

Published by Equinox Publishing Ltd.

UK: Office 415, The Workstation, 15 Paternoster Row, Sheffield, South Yorkshire
         S1 2BX
USA: ISD, 70 Enterprise Drive, Bristol, CT 06010

www.equinoxpub.com

First published 2018

British Library Cataloguing-in-Publication Data

A catalogue record for this book is available from the British Library.

ISBN-13   978 1 78179 743 3   (hardback)
          978 1 78179 744 0   (paperback)
          978 1 78179 745 7   (ePDF)

Library of Congress Cataloging-in-Publication Data

Names: Davies, Philip R., author.
Title: The Bible for the curious : a brief encounter / Philip R. Davies.
Description: Bristol : Equinox Publishing Ltd., 2018. | Includes
   bibliographical references and index.
Identifiers: LCCN 2018028182 (print) | LCCN 2018035745 (ebook) | ISBN
   9781781797457 (ePDF) | ISBN 9781781797433 (hb) | ISBN 9781781797440 (pb)
Subjects: LCSH: Bible—Introductions.
Classification: LCC BS475.3 (ebook) | LCC BS475.3 .D38 2018 (print) | DDC
   220.6/1—dc23
LC record available at https://lccn.loc.gov/2018028182

Typeset by S.J.I. Services, New Delhi, India
Printed and bound by Lightning Source Inc. (La Vergne, TN), Lightning Source UK Ltd.
(Milton Keynes), Lightning Source AU Pty. (Scoresby, Victoria).

Contents

List of Figures, Maps and Charts   vi

Part One: Bible Basics   **1**

1   Approaching the Bible   3

2   Who Wrote the Old Testament and How?   15

Part Two: Stories of Israel   **25**

3   The Old Testament and History   27

4   The Biblical Stories of Israel   34

5   A History of Ancient Israels   50

Part Three: Stories of Jesus Christ   **67**

6   Ancient Judaisms   69

7   The Gospels Story   83

8   The Acts of the Apostles   94

9   The New Testament Letters   104

10   Revelation: The End of the Story   117

Part Four: Philosophy, Ethics and Piety   **121**

11   Divination: Prophecy and Apocalyptic   123

12   Law, Wisdom and Prayer   142

Postscript   154

Index   155

List of Figures, Maps and Charts

Figure 1: The Dead Sea scroll of the book of Isaiah 8

Figure 2: Isaac prefigures Jesus, each carrying the wood 12

Figure 3: Details from Sennacherib's relief at the siege of Lachish
(British Museum) 63

Figure 4: Zodiac mosaic floor of the Bet Alpha synagogue
(sixth century CE) 76

Figure 5: Site of Qumran settlement with Cave 4 80

Figure 6: Hammurabi, the Babylonian king, receiving laws from
the god Shamash 144

Map 1: Geographical regions of Palestine 52

Map 2: The biblical view of David's kingdom 59

Map 3: The enlargement of the Hasmonean kingdom 71

Map 4: The division of Herod the great's kingdom among his sons
after his death 73

Map 5: The location of Qumran 79

Map 6: Paul's first journey (Acts 13–14) 98

Map 7: Paul's second journey (Acts 15:36–18:22) 99

Map 8: Paul's third journey (Acts 18:23–20:38) 100

Map 9: Paul's journey to Rome 102

Chart 1: Chart of Israelite scriptural history with corresponding
dates 49

Chart 2: Herod and his successors 74

Part One

Bible Basics

.

Chapter One

Approaching the Bible

WHY READ THE BIBLE?

Most Bible readers, perhaps, think the Bible contains truth, or some truth, about God, humans and the world, and teaches us this partly by describing the past and predicting the future and directing how we should live. Others dismiss it as containing myths, unscientific superstitions and old-fashioned ethical views that have little or no relevance to the twenty-first century. Additionally, for many people in our multicultural society the Bible has no historical or cultural value at all. Whether the Bible should play any role in a modern secular society is questionable. Should we bother to read it, let alone try and understand it? Having been at the centre of European (Western) culture for two thousand years, is it now of little relevance? Does it still help us to understand our culture or contribute to it? The first response to this challenge needs to be that in order to understand, appreciate and use the Bible, we do not have either to believe in it as the Word of God, nor reject it as upholding obsolete values like patriarchy, warfare, slavery, absolute monarchy or racism.

Although originating in Asia, Christianity became a state religion in the Roman Empire and determined the politics, culture and psychology of Europe and Asia, and then European global colonies. The rise and spread of Islam has not diminished that; the Qur'an is full of biblical stories and teachings, and the father of Islam is Abraham. The Bible has been, in one way or another, the common currency of all of Europe—Christian, Jewish and Muslim—and the disintegration of the Christian empire along with the growth of non-Roman Christian denominations did not dislodge the authority of the Bible but increased it. The Bible was translated and printed, and European colonization brought it across the globe. It was partly responsible for the spread of literacy everywhere.

Bible reading and Bible knowledge are now declining, like Christian belief. But its sayings and stories have become a fundamental component of Western and, indeed, of world literature. The Bible has ceased to belong exclusively to Christianity (or Judaism). Like other monuments of Christianity—cathedrals and masterpieces of music and painting—the Bible is treasured by non-believers not only as a cultural inheritance, but also as a monumental achievement of thought and imagination. A secular curiosity prompts us to consider how and why these monuments of Christianity were made, what its creators were like, and what technological and ideological values they express. But it also perceives a challenging quality. What persists, as with any great cultural monument, is an engagement between the past and the present, and between different value-systems, world-views and social psychologies. The Bible, if approached seriously, issues a challenge to respond. This book is an attempt to help inform intelligent, sympathetic and critical responses, not least by simply acquainting the reader with the contents.

The Bible is often treated as something fixed and objective. But neither as a collection of ancient writings, nor as Scripture have its form or meaning ever been stable. Or its impact. It has prompted social responsibility and care for human wellbeing. It has justified contempt, discrimination, even torture and murder. Differences of opinion over its meaning helped to cause the death of at least 3 million people in the Thirty Years' War in Europe (1618–48). Large numbers of non-Europeans died in colonial wars fuelled by biblically inspired ideologies. Even today it is used to deny women equal rights to men, and to condemn homosexuality as unnatural and evil. It has fed racist ideologies. The Bible speaks of self-sacrifice and love of others, but it also controls debate about abortion and capital punishment. Does the Bible promote any particular understanding of the value and meaning of human life? Maybe now and then, but it is the readers who must take the responsibility for what they think they understand it to say.

Among some Christian believers the Bible is believed to speak with a single voice, namely the voice of God. But should that view dictate the reading of the Bible, or should one read it first? Our modern Western values have in part derived from the Bible, but that does not mean that the Bible espouses democracy, freedom of speech, or human rights any more than it reflects modern astrophysics or bioscience. But in so many aspects of life it offers scope for critical conversation. The necessary prerequisite is to observe what it says, not what it *should* say or what we are told it says.

SCHOLARSHIP AND THE BIBLE

This book adopts a scholarly approach. But one barrier to an intelligent modern engagement with the Bible is the different degrees of understanding between biblical scholars, Christian believers, and others. The general public (including especially Christians) are likely to be familiar only with those excerpts that feature in church worship and Sunday-school education, or that have survived in a commercial and popular culture. These might include the creation of the world in six days, the Flood story, some popular psalms ('The Lord is my shepherd', Psalm 23), some odd verses of prophecy, the figures of Moses, David, Solomon, Job and Daniel, some parables of Jesus, and the stories associated with festivals like Christmas and Easter. In the nineteenth century most people knew their Bibles comparatively well. Nowadays, from large parts of both Testaments only a few verses are familiar, except to scholars or clergy. This is even more the case with the range of problems and possible interpretations that the Bible offers.

The wider public is generally well served by the media in communicating arts and sciences, despite an increasing tendency for simplification and sensationalism. An internet search on any scientific or cultural topic will generally provide a selection of sites from which a well-informed judgment can be made. None of this is the case with biblical topics. The media rarely communicate biblical scholarship, and internet search results will throw up multitudes of religiously-motivated sites which, though usually identifiable as such, tend to crowd out genuinely informed sources.

To make matters worse, experts on the Bible are not (generally) effective in explaining what they know, with very few exceptions. Such knowledge has little obvious relevance to many people, except for curiosities like the locations of Noah's Ark, Sodom and Gomorrah, the ark of the covenant, or King Solomon's mines. Biblical experts also fall into two unequal groups: those who study and those who advocate. Ever since the beginning of the scientific study of the Bible (apart from a brief period in the seventeenth and eighteenth centuries when philosophers took a professional interest), biblical scholarship has been either in the hands, or under the influence, of Christian institutions and dogmas. The Bible is nearly always studied in departments of Theology or Divinity or Religion. The majority of biblical scholars are also Christian believers—though this is less true nowadays than fifty years ago. Many are ordained priests or ministers. This is not necessarily scandalous (though imagine all academic study of the Qur'an to be in the hands of Muslim clerics). It conforms to a public consensus that the

Bible is about Christianity and that the Christian church, or, rather, various Christian churches own it, own its scholarly interpretation, and understand it best. Such a belief ensures that the Bible is taught in schools as 'religious education'. Much of what scholars write about the Bible assumes that its god really exists, that Jesus was divine and that Paul's letters communicate vital truths to us. These opinions may or may not be true but they are not scholarly. We hardly treat other scriptures this way.

In any case, public understanding of the Bible is poorly served by lack of access to the results of scholarship. Most people, for example, will not believe that the world was created in seven days, or that Adam and Eve were the first humans, or that Noah survived a universal flood in a big ship. But they may well accept most of the rest as history. They will believe the story of Jesus's birth without seeing that the two different stories of the star and wise men on the one hand, the shepherds and a manger on the other, do not easily combine. Who knows that only three gospels have a Good Friday while the fourth has a Good Thursday? Who knows the biblical book which claims life to be a meaningless and toil-ridden path to death, with only the pleasures of youth to alleviate it (Ecclesiastes)? None of these things actually demeans the Bible, which is a collection of considerable variety, parts of it rather odious (genocide), parts puzzling (Job, Revelation), parts enlightening (proverbs, parables). How we react to these parts tells us about ourselves and can promote a healthy self-criticism in a narcissistic age.

CREATING A BIBLE

This question of how the Bible was created is rarely asked, even by scholars, but to a scholarly approach it is fundamental. The answer encompasses not only the origins of the individual books but their collection and adoption as religious scriptures. For none of the authors of these writings was writing 'scripture'. The writings were created by them, but it was others who made bibles out of them.

'Bible' is in fact a misleading word: 'scriptures' is better. 'Bible' implies a single object, even a single literary work, even though the original form of the word, in Greek and Latin, was plural: 'books'. Bibles are *anthologies*. And there is no single edition of such an anthology. Non-Roman (non-Western) churches, such as the Orthodox, Eastern and Ethiopic, include other writings. The lists of scriptural contents are called 'canons', and our 'Latin' Christianity has no definitive canon. Rather, canons have been determined from time to time by church councils, resulting even in books that are deemed 'semicanonical' ('semi-word of God'?). During the long history of the Bible, some individuals even created their own scriptures. In the sixteenth century, Martin Luther wanted to remove Hebrews, James, Jude and Revelation from his German New Testament. Some individuals have even *written* their own. The first attempt we know of was in the second century CE by Marcion, who believed that the god of the Old Testament was not the same as the god of the New Testament, so he omitted the Old Testament entirely. He wrote his own gospel (a version of Luke's) and rejected some letters of Paul that he thought were not genuine (and he was probably right!). More recently, the American Founding Father Thomas Jefferson created his own 'New Testament' with a razor and glue, cutting and pasting his selection of verses from the gospels in chronological order to create a 'gospel' that matched his own opinions.

In all such cases the error was to believe that the scriptures had to speak with a single voice. This in turn stems from the conviction that the Bible is inspired and authoritative: not a human anthology but a divine manifesto. But this way of reading will result in large parts of the Bible being ignored, or their meaning twisted, in order to enable the statement 'The Bible Says', and the conclusion that what it says is what the believer thinks it should say.

For centuries the church distilled orthodoxy from the scriptures by means of exegesis (interpretation) and by selecting those parts suitable for public use. Christian bibles in the West were the possession of the few who could read Latin (and before that, Greek). Until vernacular translations were made and published, the Bible meant what the church said it meant (though clerics and educated laity disagreed often enough). But that is no longer possible: all readers have, or create, their own Bible, starting by choosing which translation, and which *kind* of translation—whether literal, idiomatic or annotated.

How did Christian scriptures come into being? They were, first of all, inherited: the earliest Christian scriptures were those of Jews. The phrase 'All scripture is divinely inspired' in 2 Timothy 3:16 can only refer to what became the 'Old Testament'; no 'New Testament' existed then. These scriptures were in Greek, mostly translated from Hebrew (with a little Aramaic). But few books had been composed in Greek. Thus, three quarters of the Christian Bible was not written by Christians. A canon of specifically Christian writings emerged alongside these, and what came to be called a 'New Testament' (composed entirely in Greek) was added to what was now known as the 'Old Testament'.

Figure 1: The Dead Sea scroll of the book of Isaiah

The Christian Bible is thus linguistically consistent; but, even more importantly, it took the form of a *codex*, a book of bound pages, while the Jewish scriptures remained in the form of scrolls until centuries later. In a material sense, the Christian scriptures, composed of many books, took the physical form of a single book, a 'Bible'.

The origin and purpose of the Jewish scriptures we can come to presently. The New Testament had a double purpose. One was to provide an authoritative literary testimony to the life, teachings and death of 'Jesus Christ'. The other was to make sense of what was now the 'Old Testament', which was the earliest Christian gospel, where the significance of Jesus Christ could be found. Jews, of course, understood (and understand) these scriptures differently.

Aramaic- and Hebrew-speaking Jews had a scriptural canon that, unlike the Greek scriptures, was already largely or entirely closed, with fewer contents and a different arrangement. Books composed in Greek were excluded. It is now fashionable to speak of these scriptures as the 'Hebrew Bible', but they did not form a single book, and their status within Judaism was not, and is not, the same as that of the Bible in Christianity.

By the fourth century, the Western Church, centred in Rome, had become increasingly Latin-speaking. The monk Jerome was instructed by the Pope to translate the Bible into Latin. His translation, known as the Vulgate, eventually—and not without opposition—became the official Bible of the whole Roman Church until the Reformation. But Jerome, as well as learning Hebrew in Bethlehem, learnt that the Hebrew and Greek scriptures did not always agree in contents or even wording. Because Hebrew had been their original language, Jerome took the view that the Hebrew texts preserved the true words of scripture and so he translated his Old Testament directly from that language. Writings that had no Hebrew equivalent Jerome proposed to leave out, but he was overruled, and under protest these were translated from Greek. Nevertheless, these have since been viewed as of lesser status, biblical but 'semi-canonical', and nowadays are often combined in a section known as the 'Apocrypha'. Martin Luther, followed by most Protestant churches, rejected them completely.

Jerome won his battle to have the Old Testament translated into Latin from the Hebrew language standardized in about the first century CE (known eventually as the 'Masoretic Text'). But the *arrangement* of the Old Testament books is not the Hebrew one. In fact, the three earliest preserved Christian Bibles, from Jerome's day (Vaticanus, Alexandrinus, Sinaiticus), all have a slightly different order of books. Even then, the order and contents had not been fixed, and modern bibles differ from all of them. But more importantly, Jerome's conviction that this Hebrew text was more 'original' has turned out to be incorrect. The discovery of the Dead Sea Scrolls in the mid-twentieth century revealed numerous Hebrew scriptural texts, some dating back as far as the third century BCE, which correspond more closely to Greek translations. The differences are not from mistakes but represent different editions, quite deliberate, and the standardized Hebrew text is not always the best. But the concept of an 'original text' is a mirage, because the writings were formed gradually, copied and recopied, and possibly in different versions simultaneously. At no point can we say that the 'original text' of, for example, the book of Jeremiah, came into existence. This realization also complicates belief in the literal inspiration of the Bible.

FROM JEWISH TO CHRISTIAN SCRIPTURES

Jewish and Christian scriptures are fundamentally different in other ways. In the 'Hebrew Bible', the three divisions of Law, Prophets and Writings attract different levels of authority and value. Preeminent are the five books of law, the *Torah*, which are read in synagogues in an annual cycle. Their coherence is a fundamental tenet, even though Judaism has not been a sacrificial religion for nearly two thousand years. Diet, circumcision, Sabbath observance, non-mixing of certain materials and festival customs continue to be observed, but the priestly, cultic aspect has vanished.

The books of Prophecy include Joshua to Kings, which contain narratives about the past, followed by books of named prophets understood by Jews as ethical teaching, illustrating and underlining the Mosaic laws. The remaining scriptural books, called simply 'Writings', have a cultural rather than doctrinal value, though five of them (Song of Songs, Ruth, Lamentations, Ecclesiastes and Esther), are each associated with a festival. The overall 'meaning' of the scriptures is, however, not a Jewish concern, and Jewish 'Biblical Theologies' are a very recent invention. It is Christians who need a meaning for these scriptures, because that meaning justifies belief in Jesus Christ.

The Old Testament, possibly following a Jewish Greek order, is divided into Law, History, Poetry (or Wisdom) and Prophecy. Law is problematic because of the negative interpretation of it in Paul's version of Christianity. How can the Jewish Law be scriptural when it has been condemned in the gospel? Yet some of it *is* still understood as binding; Christians have a day of rest, a 'sabbath', even if it has been moved from Saturday to Sunday, while the Ten Commandments are still revered as basic divine commands, and some other injunctions remain morally definitive for some Christians. The Reformer John Calvin decided to rationalise its application by distinguishing between 'ceremonial', 'judicial' and 'moral' laws. The moral laws (chiefly the Ten Commandments) are universally valid, the ceremonial laws in various ways prefigure Christ and are thus valid only until his coming, while civil (or judicial) laws, like the moral laws, are applicable to all societies, but need not be applied exactly as in the Bible, which relate only to Israel. But the Bible makes no such distinction.

The prophets are also seen very differently in the Old Testament. They do not endorse and illustrate the law, but foretell the gospel. In a certain sense, of course, the whole of the Old Testament is 'prophetic', for predictions of Christ have been discovered in the Psalms or even in the Mosaic books (for example, the 'star' in Numbers 24:17). But preeminently the prophets foresaw the coming of Jesus Christ and announced it. As the forerunner of the Messiah, David also foreshadows Jesus Christ in the Psalms.

History is separated from prophecy in the Old Testament, and it points to Jesus Christ in two ways, which are distinct but sometimes combined. One is *typological*. Here, the Old Testament story is taken as coded allusions, an allegory, rather than literally. This kind of exegesis was popular in the classical world and remained so in the Middle Ages. It can be seen in cathedral windows or private 'Books of Hours' that directed the devotional reading of the nobility. Abraham's near-sacrifice of his son Isaac in Genesis 22 prefigured Jesus's own sacrifice, with special attention drawn to the wood that each of the victims carried; there are even images in which Sarah, like Mary, is looking on. Jonah in the belly of the fish for three days pointed to Jesus in the tomb. In the letter to the Hebrews, the figure of the scapegoat bearing the people's sins in the ritual of Leviticus 16, and the priest who offers it, signify Jesus as both officiant and victim.

The other way of pointing the Old Testament to Jesus Christ is *historical*. The whole Bible divulges one god and his plan for the redemption of the world. This plan required first the election of the Jews, from whom the saviour would be born, but who would become a saviour of all humanity—and also its judge in the last days. The truthfulness of this 'sacred history' is irrelevant to the typological approach but dominated the medieval period and was dramatically represented in so-called 'mystery plays', which rehearsed the biblical story from the fall of Adam to the Last Judgment. The history they related was, however, existential as well as historical, as well as both corporate and personal. The human race fell into sin and travelled through history towards judgment. But each individual also travelled

Figure 2: Isaac prefigures Jesus, each carrying the wood

a lifetime from birth to death and beyond. Sacred history defined what it meant to be human.

In recent times, archaeology has seriously undermined the historical approach to the Old Testament, and literally-minded Christians find the typological alternative unattractive.

THE NEW TESTAMENT

The Christian gospel was at first preached from the Old Testament alone. But as the teachings spread rapidly, and the initial authority of the Jerusalem community waned, numerous accounts sprang up in other places of Jesus's teachings, his death and his exaltation. The way in which the gospel of Jesus had been spread made the growth of different versions rather easy. In the letters (including Paul's), we can see various leaders countering misunderstandings and urging loyalty to their own message. But we can also see here the emergence of local hierarchies that could control matters of belief and practice. We find references to 'overseers' (*episkopoi*, 'bishops'), assisted by 'servants' (*diakonoi*, 'deacons'), and we can trace how local churches became regional, and finally imperial, with the bishop of Rome as the head.

These structures were reinforced by a fundamental criterion of 'apostolic tradition', adherence to the teachings of the first generation of

Christian leaders who had known the earthly Jesus. (Paul was a special case: he claimed to have met the *heavenly* Jesus.) Of the inner circle of Jesus's disciples, only Matthew (the tax-collector) and John were credited with a gospel, but Luke was a companion of Paul and Mark was later said to have written Peter's recollections (see below). The letters are attributed to apostles, including James and Jude as brothers of Jesus. But the New Testament does not conceal varieties and even contradictions within the definition of an 'apostolic' tradition. Orthodoxy did not necessarily go back precisely to what either Jesus or any of his disciples taught, and differences in doctrine, especially over the person of Jesus, continued, and even now separate Western churches from others.

The Testimony of Bishop Papias (60–130 CE)

Mark having become the interpreter of Peter, wrote down accurately whatsoever he remembered. It was not, however, in exact order that he related the sayings or deeds of Christ. For he neither heard the Lord nor accompanied Him. But afterwards, as I said, he accompanied Peter, who accommodated his instructions to the necessities [of his hearers], but with no intention of giving a regular narrative of the Lord's sayings. Wherefore Mark made no mistake in thus writing some things as he remembered them. For of one thing he took especial care, not to omit anything he had heard, and not to put anything fictitious into the statements. [This is what is related by Papias regarding Mark; but with regard to Matthew he has made the following statements]: Matthew put together the oracles [of the Lord] in the Hebrew language, and each one interpreted them as best he could.

JEWISH AND CHRISTIAN SCRIPTURE: IDENTITY VERSUS BELIEF

The fundamental difference between the scriptures of Judaism and those of Christianity reflects a fundamental difference between the two religions: the role of identity and belief respectively as definitive of affiliation. Judaism came into existence as an expression of the identity of a chosen people, and the Jewish scriptures are very largely a story about 'Israel'. That identity entailed practices and stories about the past. The Law in the Jewish scriptures relates Israel's birth and its culture. The Prophets (in particular the books of Joshua to Kings) take the story further and introduce a qualifying element of Israelite identity: 'Jewishness', which was centred on the city of Jerusalem and celebrated David as its founder and ruler, on an

'Exile' and an establishment of a new 'Israel' in Judah, and on the transition from a *historical* 'Israel', represented by the kingdom. This Jewish Israel defines the identity of Jesus and his first followers.

The New Testament is a story of Jesus, but the relationship with him is mostly expressed by the word 'belief': 'faith' in Jesus Christ, who has 'saved' humans from sin and death, and from the anger and punishment of a god who is now less Jewish and more universal. 'But these are written so that you may come to believe that Jesus is the Messiah, the Son of God, and that through believing you may have life in his name' (John 20:31). The identity of the Christian god and his Messiah both derive from Judaism, but Jewish identity vanishes during the first century to the point where Jewish leaders, and even 'Jews' as a whole, are condemned—precisely because they do not believe. The Law that defines their identity also separates them from Christian identity in Jesus. No clearer demonstration is possible of the difference between the 'Hebrew Bible' and the Old Testament.

The question 'Why is there a Bible?' is, however, still far from answered. We have to press back beyond the formation of canons and try to understand how and why the writings came into being, as both 'pre-Jewish' and 'pre-Christian'. We need to seek real authors in real historical and social settings, even if their names will remain unknown to us.

Chapter Two

Who Wrote the Old Testament and How?

Here, we look at the people and processes that created the individual Jewish scriptures. We start with the processes because these point us to the authors. This includes not only initial composition or collection, but copying and recopying that always involved redrafting. (Only after these writings became 'sacred scriptures' were they retained in a fixed form.) The frequency and extent of these re-draftings can be deduced by comparing the surviving Hebrew and Greek manuscripts and analysing their structure and language. Such processes can also be directly observed within the Dead Sea Scrolls, a collection of biblical and non-biblical Jewish manuscripts, mostly in Hebrew, dating from the third century BCE to the first century CE. Among these writings we find multiple copies of the same composition preserved together, demonstrating how rapidly and frequently texts could sometimes evolve.

We refer to the contents of the Old Testament as a 'canon', but this canon is made up of other canons. When Jesus, in common with other Jews of the period, referred to the scriptures, he spoke of 'law and prophets', two distinct collections that are still preserved as divisions of the Hebrew scriptures, to which other books were later attached and called simply 'Writings'. Within these three scriptural components lie smaller 'canons', too, as will be explained presently. But we cannot talk simply of books being written at a certain date. They were, in virtually every case, shaped over several centuries, and by many people, none of whom we can identify. But we can ask what *sort* of people they were.

COLLECTIONS AND ATTRIBUTED AUTHORS

Attribution to authors gives us a clue to how pieces of writing were clustered into collections. This process occurs at several levels. The first five books contain large collections of laws—social and ritual—which have been framed by a narrative in which Moses plays the lead role. The laws come to be assigned to the Moses story, packed into a single episode of divine revelation. The story of Moses and the body of law represent the principles by which the material accumulated, and the collective names for the scrolls became 'Law' (Hebrew *torah*) and 'books of Moses'. Genesis was prefixed to this collection as a 'prequel', although it has no law and is nothing to do with Moses. Moses was at one stage associated with the mediation of all the law, but the notion that he had written the five books was later, ignoring the improbability that he could have written Genesis or the account of his own death.

Some writings were collected under the name of Solomon, especially works of wisdom (or philosophy). Given Solomon's reputation, Proverbs, Ecclesiastes, and the Wisdom of Solomon (the last of these composed in Greek) all claim his authorship. The Song of Songs, or Song of Solomon, is not philosophical, and contains words clearly written by a female, but Solomon is mentioned in it. Classifying it with 'Solomonic' scrolls was logical, and even more appropriate when it was interpreted, more philosophically, as an allegory.

The same principle can be applied to single scrolls. The composing of psalms was traditionally associated with David, and many individual psalms are ascribed or dedicated to him, even though some are actually ascribed to other authors, such as the Korahites, or Asaph, and even Moses! These in fact represent originally independent collections. But it was convenient to collect all psalms, and all collections of psalms, under David's name, and some were no doubt composed in his honour or dedicated to him. Psalms were all copied into a single scroll, and, well before the time of Jesus, David was regarded as the author of them all (and thus of the book of Psalms).

The book of Isaiah existed at some point as separate collections of sayings (clearly chapters 1–39 do not originally belong with chapters 40–66), but these collections focused on 'Zion', and thus pointed towards 'Isaiah' as a suitable figure. Thus, they were combined in one giant scroll. The 'Book of the Twelve' is, in its Hebrew (but not Greek) format, a single scroll of writings attached to different prophets. These probably began as separate texts, but at some point were combined, then copied and edited together. All the examples just given show how closely the integration of writings into scrolls and authorial attribution are part of the same process.

Who was responsible for this literary activity? They must have been people to whom we would give the name 'scribes'. Like the 'scribes' of the gospels, however, these were not mere copyists, but authors, interpreters, teachers, and thinkers. In the ancient world, these formed a small and specialized class of persons.

SCRIBES

There is no question of the Old Testament simply being the 'literature of the ancient Israelites'. Ancient Palestinians were overwhelmingly illiterate, as in any society of the pre-industrial era. An agrarian society has little use for writing, and it has been estimated that less than 5% had this ability. Of this percentage, many were interested (or capable) only in practical uses, dealing with 'documentary' or functional texts. Literary texts are a different matter. 'Oral literature' existed of course, but was created and sustained by storytellers; customs were known and reinforced by observance, rituals ingrained. Writing adds nothing. Indeed, it threatens to take away, transferring power to the elite. The growth of written texts betrays a scribal class, and this in turn a certain stage of social organization that requires written records. The two pillars of a developed society—the palace and the temple—found necessary the services of a corps of *literati*. This useful word suggests not only the ability to write, but the cultural benefits and skills that literacy facilitates. We know a lot about such scribal elites in the great kingdoms of Egypt and Mesopotamia, and the activities and interests that occupied them.

Because of their function as administrators, *literati* acquire skills of statecraft, including the techniques of bureaucracy and diplomacy. Temple scribes may, additionally, acquire expertise in sacrificial lore and religious protocol—including mythology and divination. Palace scribes would be responsible for royal propaganda, and for fiscal, calendrical and military records. But their wide knowledge of state affairs prompted them also to seek wider knowledge and understanding of what underlay their professional activities. What caused such people to produce the body of texts that became the Old Testament? The short answer can be given in three words: politics, philosophy and piety.

POLITICS

Biblical scholars, like preachers, have long accepted that the Old Testament, like the New, was born out of theological or religious motives. Commentaries on scriptural books pour out continually, clarifying their 'message' that, among the more evangelical writers, is claimed to be directly relevant to even today's world. Even where we can see the influence of political and social factors upon their writing, such as wars or social injustices, we perceive theological lessons being drawn from such events. Such a view has been standard ever since the reception of the texts as a canon. It is indeed undeniable that they deal with the Israelite god. But everyone in the ancient world believed that the gods existed and were responsible for the creation of the world, disease, famine, military success, climate, and much else. National gods dictated national fortunes; imperial gods in turn ruled over them. Gods could hardly be left out of any human calculation, and the Old Testament is not distinctive in this respect. The king of Moab, for example, a neighbour of both Israel and Judah, left an inscription explaining that his people had been conquered by Israel because their god, Chemosh, 'was angry with his people'. Why did he not think of blaming himself? The Judahite scribes certainly blamed their kings—but possibly well afterwards!

One indispensable element of scribal activity was management of the gods. It was the gods who blessed the king, and to whom the king was responsible for good governance. Divination, propitiation, thanksgiving and other rituals facilitated cooperation with them and secured their assistance. Yet the scribes, like the rulers, knew the importance of rational calculation and of learning the lessons of experience. How were these two perspectives reconciled? An illustration of how 'prophets', who were consulted about the advisability of a military enterprise, adjusted their predictions to match what they perceived as the king's intentions can be found in 1 Kings 22. After all, in the end, gods can only communicate through interpreters, and most of the interpreters were employed in the palace or the temple (the king controlled both). The story (whether fictional or not) illustrates how well its authors understood the system to work.

As a general observation, we may say that theology provided the language of politics: earthly wars were also heavenly ones, social justice was a divine commandment; kings were deposed or succeeded, defeated or victorious in battle, by the whim of deities. Later we shall explore the political agendas that drove the writing of histories and the collections of prophetic oracles and narratives.

PHILOSOPHY

It is not often considered that the Old Testament contains philosophy: the usual word for such reflections is 'wisdom'. But 'love of wisdom' is precisely the meaning of 'philosophy', and we wrongly separate the ancient Near Eastern world from the classical by not recognizing that philosophy is common to both, and the Old Testament is full of it.

The friction between rational and superstitious political responses just mentioned may have evoked cynicism among the *literati*, but philosophical reflection was called for, too. One obvious conundrum was justice. If one behaved correctly towards the gods, one should be rewarded accordingly, unless the gods were (as many thought) amoral and capricious. But in that case there would seem little point in dealing seriously with gods at all. But the same might be true of humans, and human nature had to be dealt with. The gods of most ancient mythologies are not particularly just or even moral, and the god of the book of Job betrays a dubious morality in this regard. But, like kings, gods were not entirely free of moral restraint. A king needed loyal supporters and contented subjects: gods no less. A national god without a nation is helpless. The fundamental need was to determine the gods' *interests*. A monarch's interests were to appear strong and just: mercy, rage, jealousy and benevolence were characteristics to be deployed to the best effect. But bribery was also a very useful mechanism in dealing with kings. National gods, in every respect, were the same. But the eclipse of national kingdoms in the eighth century onwards forced a reconfiguration of national gods. How were they related to imperial gods? Or, indeed, how were they related to each other? Was the emergence of monotheism, roughly in the sixth century onwards, a religious instinct or a philosophical one?

Another question: what was it to be human? How far are we like the gods, and how are we different? How different are we from beasts? For the writers of Genesis 1, we were made in the divine image, appointed to rule the earth; according to the author of Ecclesiastes, we are little different than animals.

PIETY

One's *personal* religious duty to a god can be understood in many ways. The authors of the Old Testament wished not merely to recommend piety but to explore its rationale. At least three frameworks are offered. One is contractual, between a patron deity and the client nation. But how pious is this attachment to a mutually convenient arrangement? A second mode of piety is cultic: gods are due offerings, gods need recompense for offences, gods need blandishments to secure favour. This solution is obviously attractive to the temple elites. But does it entail, or even promote, any kind of moral behaviour?

A third kind of piety emerges in many psalms that express a personal attitude, even a personal relationship towards the deity. Partly this can be understood as a historical development: from the sixth century onwards, anthropologists have theorized about an increasing individualism within all the great civilizations. But personal deities had always belonged to what we call 'household' or 'domestic' religion, and it is here, perhaps, that the roots of personal devotion lie. The writers of the Old Testament do not, however, seem attracted to such personal attachments, and may well have regarded them as idolatrous.

The Psalms were once thought to belong to the liturgy of the Jerusalem temple, and, indeed, a few of them fit well with festival occasions. But many reflect personal circumstances, whether lamenting, asking for help, or offering thanks. Few of the personal prayers will have been created ad hoc by the worshippers themselves, but may have been selected and recited by a priest on their behalf. The role of the elites in the performance of private devotions was thus considerable.

WHY AND WHEN WAS THE OLD TESTAMENT WRITTEN?

What has only fairly recently been considered by biblical scholars is that the Old Testament writings were, for the most part, not intended for public dissemination or use, but for the *literati* themselves. Alongside this is the realization that the contents do not offer a systematic account of the religious beliefs and practices of ancient Israelites and Judahites in general. During the monarchic period, the deity had a female consort, for instance, known as Asherah. Gods, including the biblical god known as Yahweh (in modern bibles, 'the Lord') or Elohim ('God'), were represented by images, temples were in every major city, shrines in every village.

Archaeological evidence suggests that the idea of a single *universal* god developed in the ancient Near East from the time of the large widespread empires, beginning with the Assyrians in the eighth century. (The Egyptian king, Akhenaton, who, in the fourteenth century promoted the cult of a single god, is probably not relevant.) It is understandable that an enlarged and integrated world, with a single 'king of kings', served by regional governors or client rulers, should imagine a divine kingdom more like an empire, with one supreme ruler and a number of officials (angels). The Judahite elite identified him with the god of Israel, but by others, including the Persian rulers, he was known by other names.

But why were these writings composed under these assumptions, and why were they preserved? Some served an official capacity, created for the sake of the rulers, or with their support. But many express criticism of kings, priests, the rich, prophets and other influential members of society. How do we explain such critical opinions from those who must have been part of the 'establishment'? After the end of local monarchy, kings could be condemned with impunity, even with the favour from an imperial regime. In the absence of royal patronage, different priestly families and guilds might also vie for power and influence, giving rise to conflicting loyalties within the *literati* also. Thus, in some books, priests are Levites (Deuteronomy), in others they are a subordinate caste of singers and other temple staff (Chronicles); in the Mosaic books, all priests are descendants of Aaron, but in Ezekiel only the 'sons of Zadok' are legitimate priests. We are presumably reading not facts but claims. To a degree, the canonized writings create the world their authors wish to inhabit.

Many of the prophetic books contain large sections condemning other nations for their bad behaviour and threatening them with divine punishment. This represents an interesting innovation in the traditional ritual of cursing your enemy in times of war, which were also times when the gods battled each other. But once the *literati* had adopted a belief in a single god, the game was not the rivalry of national deities—the existence of a large empire disposed of that option—but the pursuit of a claim to be the favoured nation of a *universal* God.

How, then, might we imagine the fairly hectic activity that preoccupied the *literati*? At any moment, in the archive or the school, any number of writings might be simultaneously updated, cross-fertilizing others. There is enough mutual referencing and counter-argument among the Old Testament texts to suggest this. As for hints of dating, a particular event or setting can explain why a book came into being (the oracles of a prophet, for example), but the final shape of a book may reflect many different contexts. Until the last fifty years, Old Testament scholars were inclined to date much of the writings to the period of the monarchies (that is, up to the beginning of the sixth century BCE) and to overestimate the extent of 'original' content, but, increasingly, such dates are being regarded rather as the starting point, and often a very small point. The reasons why the literature grew into collections and underwent revision lie mostly in later periods than those to which the books themselves refer.

It is quite possible that some texts existed, perhaps priestly practices, and collections of oracles, before the end of the monarchies. But if we are considering books, extended narratives or anthologies—that is to say, literary works—we must look mainly to Jerusalem, after its restoration as the capital of Judah in about 450 BCE. By now, the role of the scribe as a royal 'servant' had changed. There was an imperial governor's palace and a provincial temple, each with its own administrators, interests, and ideologies. National identity was no longer expressed through the monarch. There were also Israelite and Judahite communities spread across the Near East from Egypt, through Syria and Transjordan, to Babylonia; the link between a god and his land needed rethinking. But amidst all the quite intense writing and rewriting of texts during this period, one major political issue emerges that quite obviously possessed the minds of the scribes and which governs the production of a great deal of the scriptures.

JUDAH, SAMARIA AND 'ISRAEL'

The neighbouring provinces of Samaria and Judah had once been the kingdoms of Israel and Judah. The Mosaic books form a shared canon, in which the origins of an 'Israelite people' of twelve tribes—including the population of both provinces—is described. But in the remaining scriptures, a very different outlook predominates, which asserts that the real Israel exists only in Judah. This argument takes two forms in the historical and prophetic books. One is that the inhabitants of the former kingdom of Israel had disappeared forever, replaced by alien immigrants. The other is more complex: that Judah had always been the predominant tribe within Israel, and that under David, the people of Judah and Israel had united under a single dynasty, with a single capital and temple in Jerusalem. If the Samarians did not acknowledge the sovereignty of Jerusalem, they were no part of Israel. In the Judahite histories, the kingdom of Israel is either absorbed into the 'house of David' in Jerusalem, or eternally punished for its rebellion against the god of 'Israel'.

In Samaria, a province larger and less isolated than Judah, a different Israelite identity persisted; but the Samarians produced no canonized writings beyond the books of Moses. Samarians were absorbed into a kingdom of Judah that briefly flourished in the second and first centuries BCE, and thereafter became a Jewish fringe sect. In the last chapter, it was said that the Old Testament was about identity, and, for the writers, that identity was contended between Judah and Samaria. The Old Testament gives us the results of the Judahite definition of Israel.

This growing antagonism—developing somehow from an initially fraternal relationship—is what prompted the scribes of Judah, after the end of the two kingdoms, to contrast the god of Israel's punishment of Israel with his forgiveness and restoration of Judah. But alongside this nationalistic agenda stand texts that avoid Israelite identity completely and consider the ethical implications of a god who created all of humanity, and whose law is written not on tablets but in nature.

The Old Testament is therefore both smaller and larger in scale than the long-standing conventional views of scholars and non-scholars alike. On the one hand, the social circle of authorship is smaller, confined to an elite with quite specific professional duties and quite specific class interests. These writings do not describe, nor do they speak for, 'Israelites', even if popular stories and sayings have sometimes found their way in. On the other hand, the scope of interests and ideas is broader and deeper than is often appreciated, especially regarding the philosophical and political concerns that undergird the range of literary genres.

THE RELIGIONS OF 'ISRAEL' AND JUDAISM

Focusing on the 'national' conception of a 'god of Israel' and his people, rather than a universal creator deity, we can recognize two major theses on how the parties are interrelated. Each thesis is developed with its distinctive vocabulary. One is represented chiefly in the book of Deuteronomy, the other chiefly in Leviticus. The style and the ideology are signified by scholars with the letters D and P, denoting respectively 'Deuteronomistic' and 'Priestly'. Among the *literati* of both Judah and Samaria, each position strove to establish its own programme. That both are included in the canonized writings suggests that the differences did not generate mutual revulsion: rather the scribes conducted a debate. Each thesis has its own historiography: the books of Samuel and Kings, as well as parts of Joshua and Judges, clearly betray the influence of D, while the books of Chronicles reflect P. Neither of these traditions is exactly consistent with Deuteronomy or Leviticus, because within both positions there was room for difference.

These positions will be considered in Chapter 4, and here we will just introduce them briefly. Essentially, D relates Israel and its god Yahweh through the land, prioritizing social and agricultural regulations. Shared cultural identity is a key outcome. P views the cult as the medium of communication, prioritizing holiness throughout the land, with the Temple at the centre. Perhaps in these two positions we can detect two scribal 'schools', possibly the institutions of palace and temple, and perhaps, too, the profile of the Pharisees and Sadducees who appear in the New Testament, the Sadducees aligned with the priestly aristocracy and the Pharisees devoted to the Law.

But the Dead Sea Scrolls, the only Hebrew texts from Judea contemporary with the New Testament, do not easily fit into either one of these categories exclusively: they express veneration of the temple, along with holiness, but also a concern with exact obedience to the law, as they interpreted it. The books of Enoch (non-canonical in the Western church but quite influential on the worldview of New Testament writers), at the other extreme, suggest a form of Judaism in which transcendental evil forces play a role, while the importance of the law of Moses seems minimal.

We can end with the comment that just as the Old Testament authors pursued a very lively interaction of political, philosophical and social ideas, without establishing any one synthesis, so 'Judaism' itself took a number of forms, sometimes bitterly opposed, and to which, by the middle of the first century CE, Christianity was to be added. The Old Testament did not, and does not, define Judaism (or Christianity), but was born out of a process of vigorous debate. Thus, it has continued to generate disagreement, not only between Jews and Christians, but among each as well. To understand the relationship between these scriptures and the religions that venerate them, we must relinquish the idea of a foundation and accept the idea of a fountain, or, alternatively, think not of a set meal, but a menu. And while the authors are all chefs, they prefer different diets.

Part Two

Stories of Israel

Chapter Three

The Old Testament and History

THE BIBLE AS HISTORY

Almost always, 'the Bible as history' is used to mean 'what the Bible says really happened'. But before comparing Old Testament histories and modern histories, it is vital to bear in mind that 'history' can mean three things: the past, a story about the past, or the study of the past (the latter, 'History' with a capital H). The first of these is a popular but misleading usage: history is not 'the past' but rather a story about the past. No history can represent all of the past, but only excerpts within the past: periods, nations, areas or institutions. What histories do is focus on a piece of the past, but also make it *meaningful* by creating a narrative from it. 'History' is story.

But what sort of story is a 'history'? Must it relate 'what really happened'? Here, we encounter the third meaning. The discipline of History deals with our knowledge of 'what really happened'. This knowledge is gained from evidence, written and material, and is deduced by argument, because our evidence always has gaps and evidence rarely explains itself. 'What really happened' involves not merely a list of factual statements in chronological order, but facts arranged in a meaningful sequence. This involves interpretation, and explains why there can be many different histories of the same thing. More than one 'history' *may* be true, if it takes account of all the evidence. But that does not mean *any* history may be true. And, in a sense, no history can be 'true'; it can reconstruct 'what happened' but not 'what *really* happened', that is, the full description of something irretrievable.

But History is a modern discipline precisely because it needs evidence of the past, evidence that either did not previously exist, was not discovered, or was not considered. Without written materials about the past, or the material remains of archaeology, how can we have knowledge of it? When we approach the Old Testament 'as history', we need to ask what served as 'history' when these things were written. This means: what knowledge of the past was possessed by the writers, and what use was made of it?

The scribes of Israel and Judah were entrusted with records. The kinds of records that comprised 'history' we can learn better from their neighbours. From the ninth century, the Assyrians kept lists of magistrates (called *limmu*), enabling a precise yearly marker of extended time. Later, at the end of the seventh century, the Babylonians created Chronicles of events. Both are quite minimal, and did not serve the purposes of what we would call 'History'. It is not unlikely that lists of kings of Israel and Judah were also kept, recording the length of reigns and major events. There are references to 'chronicles' of the kings of Judah and Israel in the books of Kings, though the suggestion that there is lost information in them may be misleading.

Among the non-literate population, stories about the past no doubt proliferated, but without our modern distinction between 'true' and 'false', or between myth, legend, saga and genuine memory. Nothing unwritten, of course, remains for us to study, but we know a great deal about oral literature and its treatment of the past. Without a fixed chronology, and given the inventiveness of ancient storytellers, myth and legend merge with recent memory in populating a largely indeterminate past. That past sometimes explained present phenomena (deserted cities, strange rock formations, place-names), celebrated great deeds, explained social relationships, and so on. The question 'did it really happen' probably did not arise. In reading the biblical story from the creation of the universe by the word of God up to the conquest of Jerusalem by the Babylonians, ask yourself: at which point does myth become legend, and legend become 'history' in this continuous narrative? There is no hint in the Old Testament of any distinction between fiction, historical fiction, and fact.

ANCIENT HISTORIANS

It is Herodotus who, in the fifth century, coined the word *historia* ('investigation') to define his account of the past (the wars between the Greeks and the Persians, but often wandering further back), which reveals that it was based on enquiry. What earns him his title of 'Father of History' is his method of investigating, interrogating and judging: he travels widely, consulting those who have stories, often comparing them and sometimes offering his own verdict. Even so, he is quite inventive in his attribution of dialogues and conversations: he includes the supernatural (oracles are usually meaningful), he dramatizes, draws lessons and relies heavily on hearsay. His younger contemporary, the Athenian Thucydides, wrote about the war between Athens and Sparta, which he witnessed. He relied, unlike Herodotus, only on what he himself knew. Nevertheless, as he explains, he composed speeches that he deemed appropriate to the occasion rather than trying to reproduce what had actually been said. By this technique he could explain situations and motives as he understood them.

The third and last name worth mentioning is Polybius, a second century BCE Greek who was deported to Rome and participated in its wars with Carthage. His major work was a forty-volume *History of Rome*, of which only the first five books have survived. Like Thucydides, he writes very largely about what he himself witnessed, but it is worth quoting what he says (in Book 2) about history-writing in general:

> A historian should not try to astonish his readers by sensationalism, nor, like the tragic poets, seek after men's probable utterances and enumerate all the possible consequences of the events under consideration, but simply record *what really happened* and was said, however commonplace.

The idea of a sober search for facts, in opposition to the general practice of composing dramatic and edifying accounts, is therefore present before the New Testament, and Polybius's example was to be followed by several Roman historians, though 'rhetorical histories' continued to be produced. But even the most scrupulous historians could only offer the 'what happened' of recent events.

The *possible* reliability of Old Testament historians depends on where they lie in the line from Herodotus to Polybius, and how close they are to the events they narrate. The dating of the books is therefore important in assessing the degree of historical reliability that was possible. The New Testament is a different matter, and we have to begin considering the two Testaments separately. The way in which they were written, their historical context, and their purpose, are different. The answer to the question of 'what happened' may in the end be very similar, but will have to be reached by a different path.

THE OLD TESTAMENT

These writings come from a time in which hardly any ancient historians possessed reliable knowledge of the past. When not reporting events personally witnessed, like Josephus, the Jewish historian who participated in the war against Rome in 66–72 CE, writers had to rely on a few written records, often previous histories (which may or may not have been reliable) or on what people told them. It was common for historians to copy the works of their predecessors, often without acknowledgement (which we would now call 'plagiarism') and without offering any new knowledge of the past. Josephus relies largely on the scriptures, for instance, which he embellishes in order to make his story more attractive and meaningful to his readers. Entertainment was always an important factor, and Herodotus and Thucydides, we know, publicly recited their stories, designed as much to instruct and entertain as to relate 'what really happened'.

The authors of the Old Testament, educated and well-informed, had access to many kinds of literature, not only from their own people or their own kingdom. Yet their ability to gather reliable data about the past was limited. The kings of Assyria in the eighth and seventh centuries BCE had accounts of their military campaigns written down and displayed (not that most people who saw them could read them!) to boast their own power. Whether any of these were ever seen by a biblical author is doubtful, though Babylonian and Assyrian literary texts circulated across the ancient Near East and were no doubt copied. The same is probably true, to a lesser extent, of Egyptian texts.

At the same time, our *literati* were not detached from the 'oral literature' of the rest of the population. The Old Testament contains stories, such as those of Samson, Ruth, Saul, Elijah and Elisha, or Esther, that exhibit characteristics of popular legend. These have not been left alone, but made to serve the interests of the bigger story—of the fate of the kingdoms of Israel and Judah, for instance, or the 'exilic' status of Jews living abroad. The *literati* also had their own stories of life at court (Daniel and Esther, for example). The fact that every story in the Old Testament has a real-life setting in the past does not make it 'historical' but reinforces the point that the line between what nowadays we regard as 'history' and 'fiction' did not exist, because our notion of a 'real' past was not then possible.

It is obvious that a great deal of Old Testament narrative—conversations between individuals, or with God—did not take place as described. Thanks to archaeology, and especially inscriptions by neighbouring kings, reports of some major incidents and names of characters can be confirmed, as well as contradicted or corrected. Confirmations have led to the claim that the Old Testament is 'history'. But in the sense intended, 'history' is an entirely inappropriate word to be applied to these narratives. What is worse, by insisting that the value of biblical stories is their 'historicity', such claims rule out attempts to discover their true meaning and value.

What *are* they telling us? Many things: what the authors, in their ignorance, or in their limited knowledge, either believed about the past or thought they should suppose about the past, in order to explain the present, or to relate a lesson needing to be learnt. This is at least as important to us as knowing what really happened, because human behaviour and attitudes are only partly determined by what happened in the past. What is *thought* or *wished* to have happened is more significant. It is from such stories, regardless of their 'historicity', that people derive their identity, values, ethics and worldviews.

THE NEW TESTAMENT

In the New Testament, the issues are different. The New Testament books were composed in a world with a (slightly) higher degree of literacy, and the writings are, on the whole, attributable to individuals, even though they are often edited rather than composed freely. The gap between the events narrated and the dates of authorship are much shorter: Mark's Gospel is usually dated to around 70, a generation after Jesus's death, and shortly after the presumed date of Paul's death. Whereas the Old Testament books were probably gathered and edited in Jerusalem, and originally shared among a fairly small circle, the New Testament writings address a rapidly expanding network of communities. The mechanism by which stories spread and developed is thus quite different. There is no extended national story reaching far into a dim past. Instead, there is an account of the (relatively recent) life of Jesus and his first followers, bringing belief in his divinity westwards across the Roman Empire until it reached the capital. There is one common phenomenon, however. Just as the Old Testament represents the scriptures of Judah, the New Testament preserves the story of Western Christianity, that is, European, Roman Christianity. The spread of the religion eastwards has no countervailing story, even though we know that Christianity found its way as far as China. Both Testaments represent the canons of certain interests which have imposed their own history and their own authority over a story that other interests may have told differently. In this important sense, both parts of the Bible, regardless of their reliability, are at best only *someone's* history.

THE GOSPELS AND THE 'HISTORICAL JESUS'

Very few books on New Testament history start where they should: with the statement that there is no *direct* evidence outside the New Testament that Jesus ever existed. The only evidence is the fact of Christianity itself. Although several scholars have doubted Jesus's existence, it still seems more probable that such a figure did exist than that he was invented. The invention of a Jesus does not, after all, explain Christianity itself. The real question is whether such a Jesus is accurately portrayed in the gospels. Numerous modern scholars have constructed their 'historical Jesus', and with startlingly different results, including a Jewish cynic, an unorthodox rabbi, a charismatic wonder-worker, a political activist, and a prophet. The New Testament accounts themselves vary, though to a lesser degree. But Saul/Paul of Tarsus, the most significant author in the New Testament, never met the human Jesus of Nazareth, and it is uncertain whether any author of a New Testament book did, either.

For the moment, let us just focus on the gospel portrayals of Jesus in the light of our modern concerns about 'what (really) happened'. Although there are four canonical gospels, it can be argued that there are really only two basic narratives, because scholarly analysis has shown that Matthew, Mark and Luke share a common outline and a great deal of common wording. The general consensus is that Mark's Gospel was the original, and that Matthew and Luke have copied a lot of its wording while expanding its scheme, often adding details about which they nevertheless sometimes disagree. The most obvious of these is the birth stories. Mark has none, while Matthew and Luke have variant accounts, which can only mean that one or both are historically unreliable. Similarly, Mark has no appearance of the resurrected Jesus, but Matthew and Luke provide their own accounts, again different. It is unlikely that any clear, original memory of either Jesus's birth or his 'risen' appearance existed. When these three gospels are compared with the Gospel of John, more differences emerge. There is not a great deal of overlap in the teaching, and the circumstances of Jesus's life and death contain discrepancies (more detail on this is given in the next chapter).

The question that emerges from these considerations is not so much 'Did Jesus exist?' as 'Can we reconstruct a historical figure?'. Did the gospel writers aim to provide an accurate account of a life or an interpretation, sometimes using fictional narrative, of the meaning of that life? On the question of its significance, the gospels combine two perspectives on Jesus's life, or, to put it another way, on what the 'gospel' actually consists of. One is what Jesus preached, the news of the 'kingdom of God', of which he is the divine herald or even personification; the other is the redemptive death on behalf of the sins of humanity. The gospels do not reconcile these two facets but juxtapose them, without really integrating them. Paul's letters show little interest in Jesus's teaching, while the non-canonical Gospel of Thomas consists of sayings only, and such a 'sayings source' seems to have been used by both Matthew and Luke.

ACTS

The book of Acts conforms more than the gospels to what we would regard as a 'history'. There are passages using 'we' that suggest eyewitness testimony in places, but discrepancies with the letters of Paul suggest that the author was not always well informed. The sequence of events is also sufficiently vague in places to give an impression that the author did not have a clear idea of Paul's journeys. In many ways, this story conforms to the conventions of contemporary historians. The action is dramatized, there are some supernatural interventions, and numerous speeches are attributed to the major actors but composed by the author. The purpose of Acts is not innocently to chart the spread of the gospel but to champion Paul as the main architect of this mission, and to clarify that the goal of the mission was to bring the gospel from the Jewish capital to the non-Jewish one. This does not mean that the book was composed in order to establish the authority of the Roman church over the gospel. But it does explain why this book is included in the New Testament canon as the only story of the spread of Christianity.

The New Testament illustrates very well the fact that what people believe about the past is more important that what actually occurred. The two Testaments each comprise a canon whose purpose is essentially to define an identity by means of a story of the past. Yet both also show that more than one story might be told, or that one story might be told in different ways. Reading devotionally will tend to combine the stories into a single, unambiguous whole. But in a world where different cultures and identities coexist, and different stories of the past have to be celebrated and negotiated, even within Christianity, a critical approach to reading the Bible as 'history' has much to recommend it and can expand the possibilities of engagement with these texts.

Chapter Four

The Biblical Stories of Israel

A more accurate title of this chapter would be 'biblical stories of Israels', because more than one 'Israel' is going to emerge. These stories also diverge from modern stories informed by historical research, but these modern stories help us to understand better not only the realities of the world in which the Old Testament emerged, but the literary, social and imaginative world that its contents have created.

The Old Testament story begins in the five books of Moses: Genesis, Exodus, Leviticus, Numbers and Deuteronomy. Although they are known as the 'Law', laws are really only part of a narrative that describes the formation of a nation. The narrative continues in the first series of what Christian bibles call the 'Historical Books': Joshua, Judges, Ruth, 1–2 Samuel and 1–2 Kings, which describe how this Israel divides into the two kingdoms of Judah and Israel. The entire story of Israel is then retold from a new perspective in 1–2 Chronicles, and the beginning of life in Judah under the Persian Empire follows in Ezra and Nehemiah. The Apocrypha contains two accounts, 1 and 2 Maccabees, of the restoration of a Judean kingdom in the second century BCE, forming part of the Christian, but not the Jewish, scriptural story.

ISRAEL'S PREHISTORY

The birth of the 'Israel' of the books of Moses takes place when the families of the twelve sons of Jacob become a nation in Egypt, related at the beginning of the second book, Exodus. The first book, Genesis, is a prehistory that falls into two parts. Chapters 1–11 deal with how the earth is made, then populated and divided into nations living in their different lands. Chapters 12–50 tell the story of the ancestors of Israel's founder, Jacob, and of his family.

But Israel is already anticipated in the beginnings of the world. In Genesis 1, the universe is made in seven days, including a rest day. This places the sabbath as part of the order of creation. The first human pair are vegetarian, but after the Flood are permitted to kill animals and to eat them, except for the blood. This too reflects an Israelite taboo. But most of the episodes in this early history are adapted from the mythology of Mesopotamia (ancient Iraq), where the ancient civilizations included Sumer, Babylonia and Assyria. Genesis 1 is clearly modelled on the creation epic *Enuma Elish*, while the flood story is found in more than one myth. The story of the 'Garden of Eden' has no exact parallel, but contains several motifs, such as the tree of life, the loss of human immortality, and the wise snake, that are found in the Mesopotamian *Gilgamesh Epic*.

From the Gilgamesh Epic, tablet 11:
(The snake snatches the plant of immortality from Gilgamesh)

Gilgamesh spoke to Urshanabi, the ferryman, saying:
'Urshanabi, this plant is a plant against decay(!)
by which a man can attain his survival(!).
I will bring it to Uruk-Haven,
and have an old man eat the plant to test it.
The plant's name is "The Old Man Becomes a Young Man."
Then I will eat it and return to the condition of my youth.'
At twenty leagues they broke for some food,
at thirty leagues they stopped for the night.
Seeing a spring and how cool its waters were,
Gilgamesh went down and was bathing in the water.
A snake smelled the fragrance of the plant,
silently came up and carried off the plant.
While going back it sloughed off its casing.
At that point Gilgamesh sat down, weeping.

The story of chapters 1–11 of Genesis explains the conditions of human life as experienced by the majority of people: why humans die, why life is hard, why childbirth is painful, why humanity is split into different peoples and languages, and how evil came into the world. But these chapters are the product of two basic storylines that have been interwoven. So, there are two accounts of creation in Genesis 1 and 2, with seven days in the first and one day in the second, and with humans created at different points in the creation sequence. Two names, Yahweh and Elohim, are used for the deity, and two genealogies run from Adam, one through Cain and one from Seth, each leading to a Noah who collapses into a single figure as

Cain's line disappears. There are also two accounts of how humanity was scattered across the earth (chapters 10 and 11). If read closely, the story is therefore confusing. But this tells us that the narrators are not too worried about coherence. Herodotus would have included both stories separately, observing that these were alternatives, and explaining where he got them; and he might have indicated his preference. But in the Old Testament, alternatives are retained without comment; how, after all, could the author decide which was 'true'—especially if each version contained an important lesson?

Genealogies

The ancient world did not generally mark time by clock and calendar. The sun and moon controlled the measurement of the year, the sun marking the seasons, the moon the months. Beyond the annual cycle, time was hardly measured at all except by those who kept official records. But there were no universal calendars, each kingdom reckoning by the reign of the monarch. From the middle of the ninth century BCE, the Assyrians began to compile the name of officials called *limmu*, allowing each year to be identified by name, and the past to be measured by the lists (the Romans did likewise, with the names of consuls). King-lists were also kept, and from almost the very beginnings of recorded human history in Mesopotamia we find kings with extraordinarily long reigns, similar to the long human lifespans in the early chapters of Genesis. These figures are not at all reliable, though some of the kings did exist.

Within families, generations provide a rough sense of time passed, but a generation is not a fixed period, and in the Old Testament forty years seems to have been used as an average (forty years of wandering in the desert was enough for a generation of Israelites to die out, as we are told in Numbers). The main use of genealogy was relational, not chronological: genealogies marked not only genuine kinship but social or political alliance or enmity: allies or neighbours became 'brothers'.

Genesis uses genealogies in various ways. In chapter 5, they seem to provide a chronological framework. We are given not only the length of life of each character but the years before the birth of the son who represents the next generation. The data enable a precise chronology to be constructed, though the figures given are schematic. In chapter 10, the function is geographical, not temporal: all the nations of the earth are derived from the three sons of Noah, and spread out into their respective lands. Later still, the genealogy of Abraham generates a map of the nations living in Palestine, while the twelve sons of Jacob are constructed as the ancestors of Israelite tribes. But here the mother's identity also carries a code. Joseph and Benjamin, for example, are born from the favourite wife, Rachel, suggesting a close affiliation between the tribes of the 'house of Joseph' and Benjamin. A further example of how genealogies are codes for something else is found in Matthew and Luke. Matthew 1 traces Jesus's descent to Abraham, and includes the female characters Tamar and Ruth, because the link to Jesus is via Mary, while Luke 3 goes back, via Joseph, to Adam, and even one more, since Adam is 'son of God'. Attempts to reconcile these diverging lists as if they were intended literally misses the point.

In Genesis 12, Israel's own prehistory commences with a divine call to Abraham, who, though originating from Ur in Mesopotamia, is living in Syria. He is to occupy a land promised to him and his descendants, and to receive a blessing. (These two need to be kept separate.) The land, which turns out to be Canaan (Palestine), will be occupied by his descendants: Ishmael (Nabatea), Jacob (Israel), and Esau (Edom), while across the Jordan, Ammon and Moab are also related through Abraham's nephew, Lot. Only the Philistines are left out, because culturally they are different from the other, Semitic inhabitants. The blessing, however, goes to the younger sons (Isaac and Jacob) and focuses on Israel. Abraham seems careless of land and blessing. He attempts to dispose of two of his sons, Ishmael and Isaac, and to settle outside Canaan. But the family finally settles in the land, until the eleventh of Jacob's sons, Joseph, who incurs his brothers' envy, is sold off by them and enslaved in Egypt. But he prospers there and the whole family eventually joins him. By the end of Genesis, Jacob's family is about to become the people of Israel. But in the process, Abraham has deceived Sarah, Jacob, his father Isaac and his brother Esau, while Joseph's brothers sell him off, and Joseph later deceives them too. The writers have no intention of glorifying these characters.

BECOMING A NATION

Descent alone does not define a nation. The story now brings Israel to the promised land of Canaan. The now numerous descendants of Jacob are enslaved by the Egyptian king but introduced by Moses to their god, Yahweh. Moses is given a dramatic birth story borrowed from an account of the semi-legendary Sargon, king of Agade in Mesopotamia. The eventual escape of the Israelites is effected with the aid of miracles: Yahweh inflicts plagues and other disasters on the Egyptians, and finally causes the waters of the Reed Sea (not the Red Sea) to part and close, drowning the pursuers. The people then trek towards Mount Sinai, which Moses ascends to receive Israel's laws from Yahweh. The story now progresses slowly since the laws are quite extensive, occupying the second part of Exodus, all of Leviticus and some of Numbers. Many of the cultic laws are addressed to Moses's brother, Aaron, who will be the ancestor of all the priests. The people are generally not happy with their release: they ask Aaron to make them a golden idol of a calf while Moses is on the mountain, and during the onward march to Canaan they frequently grumble and even rebel. The Israelites are disobedient and ungrateful from the outset, and because of their disobedience must spend forty years wandering before a new generation can occupy the land, and even Moses may not enter. As in the stories of Abraham and his sons, the narrators paint a less than glowing portrait.

But at the end of Numbers, after vanquishing those who oppose their progress, the nation arrives in Moab, east of the Dead Sea, and Moses makes a speech in which the previous events, and the laws, are repeated, though with some variation. This speech forms the book of Deuteronomy. Then Moses dies, in an unknown location, having seen the land but not having entered it.

Sargon of Agade (ca. 2300 BCE) tells of his birth

Sargon, the mighty king, king of Agade, am I.
My mother was a changeling, my father I knew not.
The brother(s) of my father loved the hills.
My city is Azupiranu, which is situated on the banks of the Euphrates.
My changeling mother conceived me, in secret she bore me.
She set me in a basket of rushes, with bitumen she sealed my lid.
She cast me into the river which rose not (over) me.
The river bore me up and carried me to Akki, the drawer of water.
Akki, the drawer of water, lifted me out as he dipped his e[w]er.
Akki, the drawer of water, [took me] as his son (and) reared me.

ISRAEL DEFINED BY ITS LAW

The narrative and the laws in these books belong together. The first tells how Israel came to be, and the second defines what it is supposed to be. But we encounter three different utopian definitions. Putting them together within the story is a brilliant way of challenging the reader to see that Israel might be constructed in more than one way, possibly reflecting a period of composition when defining Israel was a contested exercise. The three utopias are described in Leviticus, Numbers and Deuteronomy. Though set in the wilderness, they look forward to life in Canaan.

Leviticus is not easy for the citizen of a modern secular society to understand. The minutely detailed concerns of the first nine chapters—priests and sacrifices—seem distant not only from us, but probably even from most ancient Israelites. But in Leviticus's view, the priests and their rituals are central. They mediate the relations between Israel and its deity, which is crucial for Israel's continuing existence. Priests control Israel's vital and distinctive quality—holiness—without which humans and God cannot live together nor even communicate. So everything is mapped with invisible contours of holiness, cleanness and impurity. Some objects and persons are always unclean (cloven-hoofed animals, lepers, menstruating women, corpses): Israelites can become clean by various means of purification, mostly washing and sacrificing. There is also a moral realm of uncleanness, which can be entered through, for example, idolatry, or forbidden sexual relations. Guilt can be atoned for individually, but annually on the Day of Atonement (chapters 16 and 23), when the whole population can shed its accumulated guilt, whether deliberate or accidental. The land can also become unclean if it is not rested every seventh year (chapter 25) and if its produce is not tithed. According to chapter 26, a major reason for the deportation of the nation is for the land to 'enjoy its sabbaths' while its inhabitants repent their sins. We can describe the Israel of Leviticus as a hierocratic society.

Numbers is quite different. It opens with a census of those 'able to go to war', from which point the nation is an army on the march towards a destination to be conquered, living off the terrain and constantly on the alert for any attack. The god Yahweh is a general leading his troops: in the form of a cloud when on the march and otherwise in the general's tent. So when the ark is about to be carried forward, Moses says 'Arise, Yahweh, let your enemies be scattered and your foes flee before you', and when it stops, 'Return, Yahweh of the massed armies of Israel' (10:35-36).

The families and tribes of Israel are configured as military units, providing specified numbers of young men to fight, and the story carries a very military emphasis on discipline, obedience and loyalty to the leader. Rebellion is frequent (see chapters 14, 17 and 20) and harshly punished. The Israel of Numbers might be classified not so much as a military dictatorship but as a warrior nation.

In Deuteronomy, we find an Israel that corresponds better to modern Western ideals. Its religion is a contract ('covenant') between Yahweh and his people, with mutual obligations. The big print stresses keeping away from 'Canaanite nations' and certain other foreigners and not worshipping their gods in return for security in the land. The small print is in maintaining a righteous and just society that protects the poor and constrains the powerful: slaves and women are less badly treated than in many of the legal norms of the time. The laws are written down in a book, which even the king will be obliged to read and to which he will be subject (17:18-20). Authority is decentred: the cult and priesthood are hardly mentioned; Levites and elders exert control locally. The designated place of sacrifice is also a place of pilgrimage, where Israelites go on their great festivals of Unleavened Bread and Passover, Weeks (Pentecost) and Booths (Tabernacles). These are occasions for offering firstfruits (crops and herds are part of Deuteronomy's 'cult') but also constitute moments of national remembrance of Israel's foundation story. This Israel is a constitutional monarchy, but not a democracy. It is a theocracy.

None of these three ideal Israels was fully realized, but out of the ethic of holiness and the notion of covenant, a Judaism without a temple or a functioning priesthood was finally created. The militant ideal was not lost, however: the story of the conquest of Canaan fits it very well, while in Judah's wars with Syria and with Rome, militancy was enthusiastically embraced by nationalist zealots.

OCCUPYING THE LAND OF CANAAN

The Israel of the books of Moses resides in scriptures shared by Judaism and Samari(t)anism, who together make up the twelve tribes. But the remainder of the biblical history is conveyed in Judahite-Judean scriptures and reflects the sometimes torturous process by which 'Israel' becomes either confined to Judah or centred on Judah. (There is a 'Samaritan chronicle', mostly about Joshua, but from a medieval date.)

The books of Joshua and Judges describe how Canaan is taken, assigned to the tribes, and defended from invaders. First, spies are sent to Jericho, and concealed by Rahab, a prostitute who acknowledges Yahweh and asks for her family to be spared in return. She is the first recorded convert in the Bible and becomes an ancestor of Jesus in Matthew 1:5, an example of faith in Hebrews 11, and justified by her deeds in James 2. The importance of her story is that the distinction between 'Israelite' and 'Canaanite' is not purely ethnic, but also depends on religious allegiance.

There are generalized statements about the conquest of Canaan, but descriptions of only a few parts. Jericho's walls miraculously collapse, and in accordance with Yahweh's law, all living things are slaughtered, except for Rahab and her household. The city of Ai is the next target, but initial attempts fail because an Israelite called Achan had withheld booty from Jericho that should have been devoted to Yahweh. He is discovered and, along with his family, is slaughtered, becoming the opposite of Rahab: a faithless Israelite treated like a Canaanite. This lesson is more important than any historical questions.

As Joshua becomes old, land still remains to be taken and he is commanded by Yahweh to divide the territory in detail among the tribes, and most of the rest of the book defines these borders. The climax of the allotment process is a great covenant ceremony at Shechem, where Israel promises to be faithful to its god.

But when Joshua dies, Judges begins with each tribe having to win its own lands. No unified conquest had occurred, then. The tribal efforts are also mostly unsuccessful—so no 'conquest' at all! Only Judah succeeds entirely in winning its territory; other tribes have to live alongside Canaanites, and all have to defend what land they have from invaders, as they do when they regularly depart from Yahweh. But then they cry out for help, and Yahweh sends a series of 'judges', who perform heroic deeds, like Ehud, Gideon and Samson. The editors of this book have combined stories about these local heroes into a cycle and created a scheme in which all Israel is ruled continuously by a succession of judges. A 'period of the Judges' is an artificial construct, though the individual stories may preserve some genuine tribal memories.

The system finally breaks down in civil war, in which the tribe of Benjamin is defeated (just!) by the other eleven, led by Judah. Their women having been wiped out, the men of Benjamin capture new wives during a festival at Shiloh. 'In those days', concludes the book, rather ambivalently, 'Israel had no king. Everyone did what they considered to be right' (or 'did as they pleased'). But kingship had already been claimed by one judge (Abimelech) and refused by another (Gideon). This is about to change in the books of Samuel.

MONARCHY

The entire history of the monarchies is told in the books of Samuel and Kings (or 1–4 Kingdoms in the Septuagint). The last of the judges, Samuel, is asked by the people for a king 'like the other nations'. He resists, but Yahweh tells him to relent. Saul, from the tribe of Benjamin, is chosen (there is more than one account of this), but he falls out of divine favour and Samuel anoints David, who joins Saul's court, killing Goliath and pacifying Saul's 'evil spirit' with his music. David marries Saul's daughter and befriends his son Jonathan, but then finds himself being hunted down by the jealous Saul.

During these events, Israel's makeup changes in a curious but highly significant way. The Israel of the twelve tribes splits into two 'houses' of Judah and Israel, with Saul apparently ruling only over the 'house of Israel', while David belongs to the 'house of Judah', although he enters Saul's service and becomes an heir apparent by marrying Saul's daughter and befriending his son. After Saul and Jonathan die in battle with the Philistines (about whom we are told very little, but we know had settled on the coastal plain of Canaan), David becomes king of Judah. Then he contends for the throne of Israel with Saul's son, Ishbaal, and finally succeeds in ruling both kingdoms. David captures Jerusalem and establishes it as his capital. He brings the ark there and is promised that Yahweh will 'build him a house'. 'House' can mean both a dynasty and a temple, and David does found a dynasty, though the temple is left to Solomon to build. David embarks on a series of wars to enlarge his kingdom, but the union lasts only under David and successor Solomon. The point of creating this 'double kingdom' is to establish a political identity for twelve tribes while keeping the houses of Israel and Judah distinct, and establishing Jerusalem and David's line as the legitimate centre.

In 2 Samuel, the plot focuses on David's domestic affairs, and turns into something of a soap opera. David gives up going to war, falls for Bathsheba and has her husband, Uriah, killed in order to marry her. Amnon, David's eldest son, rapes his sister, Tamar, and is forgiven by his father but not by his third son, Absalom, who has Amnon killed and then challenges David for the throne. David retreats from Jerusalem, but Absalom is killed by David's general, Joab. Bathsheba bears David a son, who dies as a divine punishment, but their second child, Solomon, becomes David's heir. So the story of David's life gives us two characters: the ruthless but upright young warrior, then the weak and devious king and father. David's career ends on a low note, too, with his plan for a census resulting in a plague on all the people, arrested only by his offering a sacrifice.

Solomon likewise exhibits a double character. At first he seems the epitome of the magnificent ruler, ruthless in seizing the throne and taking care of his rivals, but blessed with the gift of wisdom from Yahweh. He gains huge wealth, mostly from trade, enticing a visit from the queen of Sheba, and commissions an impressive temple from Hiram, king of Tyre. But his marriages to several foreign women—normally part of a successful king's repertoire—attracts him to their gods, for which he is told that his kingdom will be divided after his death and eleven tribes (that is, the 'house of Israel') will be torn from his realm. In some ways an ideal ruler, then, Solomon commits the worst offence by worshipping other gods, consolidating his kingdom, but also bringing about its dissolution. An Israelite called Jeroboam had been appointed to help oversee Solomon's forced labour programme, but was told by the prophet Abijah that he would be given ten tribes taken from Solomon's kingdom. Solomon's enmity causes Jeroboam to flee to Egypt.

When Solomon's son, Rehoboam, is rejected by the 'house of Israel', Jeroboam returns and is crowned as their king, leaving one tribe to Rehoboam. But now we must ask why the tribes under Jeroboam are sometimes numbered ten and sometimes eleven. It is hinted that the tribe of Benjamin joined with Judah. Given the previous enmity between them, this seems very unlikely, but the ambiguity conceals an important clue for the historian, which we can follow up later. The authors of Kings, at any rate, now use 'Israel' exclusively of Jeroboam's kingdom: it no longer refers to a twelve-tribe nation.

But, this being a Judahite story, Jeroboam's kingdom, born of rebellion against David's house, is criticized from the outset. Jeroboam installs two royal temples at the extremities of his kingdom, Dan in the north and Bethel in the south, their cult denounced as idolatrous. A whole history of idolatry results, leading eventually to the downfall of the kingdom. In between, a long section is devoted to the activities of the prophets Elijah and Elisha, who challenge Israelite kings and support a coup by the enthusiastic Yahweh-worshipper, Jehu. The verdict on Jehu is ambiguous: he 'wiped out' the worship of the god Baal but 'was not careful to follow the law of Yahweh the god of Israel with all his heart; he did not turn from the sins of Jeroboam, which he caused Israel to commit' (2 Kings 10:31).

The histories of the two kingdoms are interlinked with cross-references to the reigns of their monarchs. All of these are judged purely by their allegiance (or lack of it) to Yahweh, their worship of other gods and their toleration of places of worship other than Jerusalem. Jeroboam's successors (even Jehu in the end) 'do what is evil in the sight of Yahweh', while in Judah, some kings are righteous, but many are not. Two kings stand out as models of good behaviour, each instituting religious reforms: Hezekiah, whose reign coincided with the fall of the kingdom of Israel, and Josiah, who ruled a century later as the Assyrian Empire was giving way to the Babylonian.

After the fall of the kingdom of Israel, its population is deported, and foreigners brought in. Although the worship of Yahweh continues there,

the people of the former kingdom of Israel are deemed to be lost forever, and the new immigrants are not descendants of Jacob, so not really
Israelites. Just over a century later, the kingdom of Judah is also brought
to an end, this time by the Babylonian king, Nebuchadnezzar. He deports
the upper strata of the people, but does not introduce foreigners. However,
there is some immigration from surrounding areas. A new ruler, Gedaliah,
a Benjaminite, is installed in Mizpah, but assassinated by a pro-Davidic fac-
tion, and the land is emptied. The books of Kings end not in Judah, but with
a note that the deported king, Jehoiachin, was pardoned, released and 'sat
at the king's table' until he died. If a note of hope for the future is sounded
here, overall the verdict on native monarchy is negative—as at every other
stage of Israel's history. The rulers of both kingdoms, despite the urgings
of prophets, had not heeded the demands of Yahweh, and left an uncertain
future for their subjects.

AN ALTERNATIVE 'HISTORY OF ISRAEL'

We now encounter a second story of Israel in the books of Chronicles. Its
authors did not accept a story according to which Israel had become per-
manently divided. It had to be retold from the beginning. But for the time
before David, we are given little more than a set of genealogical notes,
starting from Adam. The narrative properly commences with David's
assumption of kingship. There is no 'house of Judah' and 'house of Israel',
only one people and one kingdom. David's 'houses', dynasty, and temple
remained, in the Chronicler's view, the heart of Israel. A split in the time
of Rehoboam is described, but the resulting kingdom is not mentioned
again. Indeed, we read in 1 Chronicles 9:3 that 'some of the people of Judah,
Benjamin, Ephraim and Manasseh lived in Jerusalem' and, after the fall of
Samaria, Hezekiah, the king of Judah, is said to invite the Israelites outside
Judah to participate in his Passover:

> So they decreed to make a proclamation throughout all Israel, from Beer-
> sheba to Dan, that the people should come and keep the passover to Yahweh
> the God of Israel, at Jerusalem; for they had not kept it in great numbers as
> prescribed. Couriers went throughout all Israel and Judah with letters from
> the king and his officials, as the king had commanded, saying, 'O people of
> Israel, return to Yahweh, the God of Abraham, Isaac, and Israel, so that he
> may turn again to the remnant of you who have escaped from the hand of
> the kings of Assyria.' (2 Chronicles 30:5-6)

Note that this description cannot avoid referring to 'Israel and Judah' or alluding to the Assyrian conquest. Reality has to break through somewhere! But a little later, in 2 Chronicles 34:9, we read of a collection for the Jerusalem temple:

> They came to the high priest Hilkiah and delivered the money that had been brought into the house of God, which the Levites, the keepers of the threshold, had collected from Manasseh and Ephraim and from all the remnant of Israel and from all Judah and Benjamin and from the inhabitants of Jerusalem.

The Israel of Chronicles is founded on the temple which, according to the authors, David designed and built, and wrote the liturgy of. And so, unlike the Israel of Kings, this one can survive political collapse. The last verses of 2 Chronicles thus look forward:

> In the first year of King Cyrus of Persia, in fulfilment of the word of Yahweh spoken by Jeremiah, Yahweh stirred up the spirit of King Cyrus of Persia so that he sent a herald throughout all his kingdom and also declared in a written edict: 'Thus says King Cyrus of Persia: Yahweh the god of heaven has given me all the kingdoms of the earth, and he has charged me to build him a house at Jerusalem, which is in Judah. Whoever are among you of all his people, may Yahweh their God be with them! Let them go up.'

Cyrus is the divinely appointed king and temple builder, the new David, and under imperial rule, the story of Israel can continue. It is not always appreciated, even by scholars, that Chronicles is the story of a different Israel, though still clearly from a Judahite perspective. Indeed, it goes one better than Kings: the united Israel of David is not in the past, a failed political initiative, but a vision of the future in which the two provinces of Judah and Samaria unite in loyalty to Jerusalem.

THE 'POST-DEPORTATION' GAP

The next stage of the story offers a lesson that what is *not* said in a history may be as significant as what *is* said. It has already been noted that any 'Israel' based in Samaria has been negated, in different ways, by both the Kings and Chronicles stories. But there is also a large chronological gap between the end of the kingdom of Judah and the edict of Cyrus. A brief account at the end of Kings notes the fate of those left behind in Judah, but ends with an empty land. Chronicles likewise has an empty land, but with the explanation that seventy years of 'rest' were needed for it to regain the fallow 'sabbatical' years it should have enjoyed but did not (calculated as 70 × 7 = 490 years of occupation followed by 49–50 years of exile). For a long time, Judah was indeed 'empty' even for historians, and only in recent decades has interest developed in this piece of history. But for the biblical story, a Judah without Jerusalem was indeed 'empty', an era to be forgotten.

JUDAH AS ISRAEL

Chronicles is followed by the books of Ezra and Nehemiah, and because the beginning of Ezra recapitulates the end of Chronicles, the books used to be treated as the work of a single author. But Ezra and Nehemiah tell the story of yet another 'Israel'. The first six chapters of Ezra narrate how the 'leaders of Judah and Benjamin' in Babylonia prepare to go to their ancestral homeland and rebuild the temple in Jerusalem. But there are 'enemies of Judah and Benjamin' who, initially offering to help, are rebuffed and so try to hamper the work by appealing to the Persian king, Artaxerxes. The king issues a ban on further building which is later revoked by Darius and the temple is finally built. But exactly who the 'enemies' are is not clear.

Ezra, a scribe 'skilled in the Law', appears only in chapter 7, where his activities are initially described in the first person, as if taken from a memoir. He comes from Babylonia, along with other immigrants, with a royal commission to take gifts for the temple and to impose the law of his god. On finding that intermarriage with outsiders has taken place, he utters a long prayer of remorse and orders the wives to be put away, along with any children. A list of the priests who had offended in this way brings the book to an end.

Nehemiah's story also begins in the first person, again as if a memoir. A cup-bearer to Artaxerxes, he asks to be sent to Jerusalem to 'rebuild it' and appears to have been installed as governor of the province. Like Ezra, he meets with local opposition, which this time is identified: Samarian leaders (Sanballat and Tobiah), Ammonites, Arabs, and 'Ashdodites' (possibly a derogatory term for indigenous Judahites). He sets to (re)building the city wall, and a quite detailed description of its course and its gates is supplied. So is the continued activity of his opponents. Then Nehemiah conducts a census, which produces another list of all those who came from Babylonia and their original home towns. Some economic issues are dealt with, but while the wall is being completed, the city is without housing.

In a central scene (Nehemiah 8), Ezra and Nehemiah appear together for the only time. This is strange given their similar leadership roles and apparently overlapping dates (during the reign of Artaxerxes). This occasion is the autumn New Year festival that includes the Feast of Booths and the Day of Atonement. The 'book of the law' is brought by Ezra, and read out; there is prayer and confession. Levites recite a blessing that summarizes Israel's history, reminding the people that, because of the sins of their ancestors, 'we are slaves today'—that is, subjects of a foreign king. At the conclusion, a written pledge is produced to keep separate from foreigners, including the 'people of the land', and to bring firstfruits to the temple. The signatories to this document are listed.

The first-person narrative resumes as Jerusalem is repopulated by moving a tenth of the people into the city (apparently the point of the earlier census). A ceremonial procession around the walls follows and, finally, Nehemiah orders the gates of the city closed on the Sabbath, to exclude foreign traders. Judahites who had married foreign women are again castigated.

There are many curiosities in the biblical accounts of the revival of Jerusalem. The earliest Christian bibles contain a different version of this part of Israel's story, in a book known as 1 Esdras. This book contains most of what is in Ezra, plus the last two chapters of Chronicles, as far back as the reign of Josiah, and the story in Nehemiah 8 of the great assembly, in which Ezra plays a role. The book also features an additional episode at its centre, after Ezra 4, known as the 'Story of the Youths'. This episode seems to carry the book's main theme, which is a celebration of Zerubbabel ('seed of Babylon'), whom the book of Ezra describes as the leader of those returning from Babylon to rebuild the temple. He is named here as a governor of Judah and, according to 1 Chronicles 3:17, was the grandson of the exiled king of Judah, Jehoiachin/Jeconiah. This centerpiece features a court contest in which Zerubbabel is the winner and is consequently invited by the king to lead Jews back to their homeland. The existence of this book (in Greek only) gives further insight into the freedom with which the scriptures have fashioned the past, and especially this bit. Many different versions have been juxtaposed, and others combined.

In particular, let us consider the existence of stories about two different people, Ezra and Nehemiah, fulfilling similar functions, apparently working at the same time, but meeting only once. There is a strong likelihood that they arose as alternative stories of how life resumed after

Judahites returned from Babylonia. If so, they express different priorities and interests. The Nehemiah story bears a political agenda, building the city walls and addressing economic problems. The Ezra story is about loyalty to the Law and the character of the community. The numerous lists in both books might suggest that the stories were developed by groups who traced their ancestry back to Babylonian deportation ('exile') as a mark of their credentials. A new definition of 'Israel' sticks out here—not just 'Judahites' but *returning Judahites*. The Samarians, formerly the populations of the kingdom of Israel, are not only no longer Israelites, but opponents. Interestingly, this new 'Israel' is like the old 'Israel' of Genesis to Deuteronomy. It is like Abraham's family too: immigrants, and the indigenous population is repeatedly rejected and displaced. Another feature to take note of: the great founding event of the twelve-tribe Israel, the exodus and lawgiving, whose memory is shared by Judah and Samaria, is now overlaid by another, purely Judahite one, the 'return from exile'.

FOREIGNERS

The 'History' section of the Old Testament contains also the books of Ruth (between Judges and 1 Samuel) and Esther (after Nehemiah). Ruth's inclusion no doubt arises from its links to David's ancestry, a connection that might have been added later to the ending. Otherwise, this story is about migration and intermarriage. A Judahite called Elimelech takes his wife, Naomi, and his sons to Moab, where the sons marry Moabite wives. When Elimelech and his sons die, Ruth, one of the wives, volunteers to migrate to Judah herself with Naomi. Ezra and Nehemiah may have opposed intermarriage, but like Rahab from Jericho, here is another foreign woman who benefits her adopted people. The tale of Esther's is harder to explain. It may well arise from the feast of Purim, but it is a revenge tale on two levels. The Jews are granted the right by the Persian king to massacre their enemies, but the hero, Mordechai, who is from the tribe of Benjamin, also gains revenge on the villain Haman of the fictional 'Agagites'. Mordechai's ancestor, King Saul, had failed to execute the Amalekite king, Agag (1 Samuel 15), as a result of which Yahweh turned against him. But the most striking feature is that the heroine marries the Persian king! Like Joseph and like Daniel, Esther features Jews succeeding in a foreign court; but while, like the other heroes, she uses worldly wisdom, Esther exploits her sex appeal too.

The inclusion of two (sometimes four) Maccabean books (relating to the second century BCE) into the Old Testament serves the useful purpose of filling some of the gap between the Persian era and the period of the New Testament. But they belong to a story of Judah rather than of Israel and we can consider this story later within a description of early Judaisms.

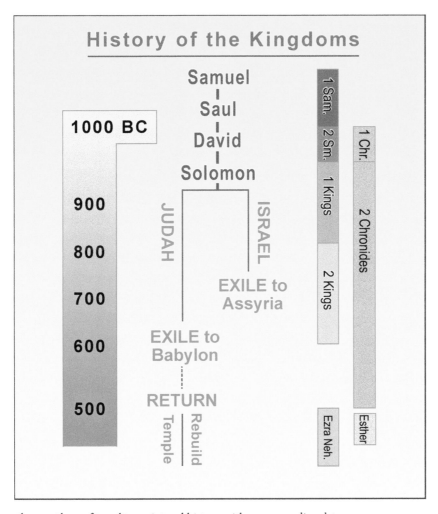

Chart 1: Chart of Israelite scriptural history with corresponding dates

Chapter Five

A History of Ancient Israels

The land of the Old Testament runs from the Mediterranean Sea eastwards to the Jordan Valley, and from the borders of modern Syria and Lebanon as far as Egypt and the Sinai Peninsula. Ancient writers called this land many names, including part of Syria, Canaan, Retenu and Palestine. It has four geographical zones: (from west to east) the coastal plain, lowlands, highlands and the Jordan Valley. The Jordan Valley, including the Dead Sea and the lake of Galilee, is part of the Great African Rift and forms the lowest point on the earth's surface. On a map, it may seem a major barrier but the river can in fact be crossed at may points quite easily on foot. Beyond it lies the Jordanian plateau.

This piece of land formed a land bridge between the two great civilization centres of Egypt and Mesopotamia. The main routes ran north-south from Egypt along the coast as far as the Carmel range, cutting east through to the plain of Jezreel or Esdraelon, then turning north at the Jordan to Damascus and to the Euphrates river. Another road linked the Red Sea and Damascus, running east of the Jordan Valley. A route over the highlands was hardly used for long-range transport, because the valleys here run east-west and are quite steep, especially in the south. East-west a route ran across to the Red Sea, linking the Mediterranean with Arabia. Various roads also ran along the valleys from the coast to the highlands. These features are shown on the maps below.

In the Late Bronze Age (1550–1250 BCE), this land had consisted of small city-states under Egyptian domination. This system collapsed for several reasons, and the history of Palestine relevant to the Bible begins with that collapse. The arrival of the Philistines on the coast precipitated Egypt's withdrawal of permanent control and permitted the creation of a number of small kingdoms. The coastal plain was occupied by Phoenicians, and the Philistines established five cities in the plain and the lowlands. In the highlands and across the Jordan Valley, territorial kingdoms emerged. West of the Jordan these were Israel and Judah; across the Jordan were Moab and Ammon; Edom lay south of the Dead Sea; further north was the kingdom known in the Old Testament as 'Aram', centred in Damascus.

Bible atlases reproduce the biblical image of a stable geographical disposition, but these political units fought for more territory: the Philistines vied with Israel for the lowlands, Aram and Israel fought for supremacy in Lower Galilee, and Israel sought to expand east of the Jordan. Territory was defined by control, not by fixed borders, and it fluctuated until the great empires of Assyria, Babylonia and then Persia determined provincial boundaries—and local warfare largely ceased.

These kingdoms then mostly became provinces. The Assyrian Empire gave way to the Babylonian towards the end of the seventh century, and the Babylonian to the Persian just under a century later. The Persians then ruled for 200 years, giving way to Alexander of Macedon and his successors—first the Ptolemies in Egypt (312–194), then the Seleucids in Syria. A brief Judean kingdom was created in 140, conquering much of Palestine and lasting until Rome's intervention in 63. Herod the Great ruled much of Palestine as the 'king of the Jews', under Roman patronage, but under his successors the land was partitioned and a much smaller Judah was returned to direct Roman rule. After two revolts in 66 and 132, an officially post-Jewish province of Syria Palaestina was created. For the last 2000 years, that has been the name of the land.

Given these geographical, strategic and political factors, and as its history proves, Palestine would never contain a major power, or not for long. It was an international corridor, guaranteeing it a volatile history during which the political and cultural influence of the east gradually gave way to those from the west. But, by then, east and west were mingling closely.

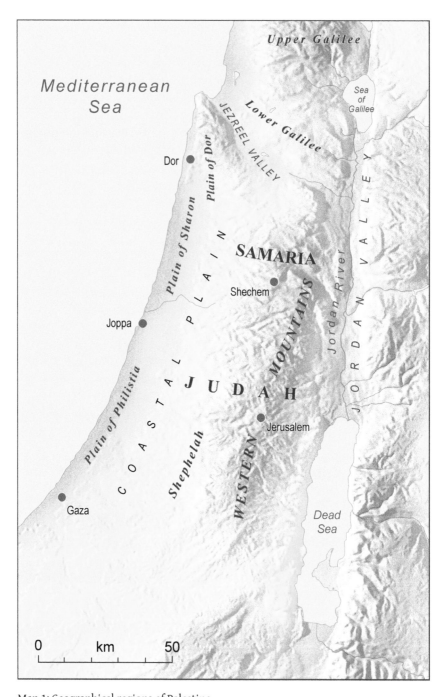

Map 1: Geographical regions of Palestine

1550–1200	City states under Egyptian control.
1200	New Israelite (?) settlements appear in highlands. 'Sea Peoples' settle on coastal plain. Egyptian control dwindles.
ca. 950–722	Kingdom of Israel established under 'house of Omri', Judah under 'house of David', subject to Israel and/or Aram.
722	Assyrians destroy kingdom of Israel, create province of Samaria. Population transfers.
612	Assyrian Empire falls to Medes and Persians.
586	Babylonians destroy kingdom of Judah, create province of Judah. Deportation of upper classes. Capital moved to Mizpah.
539	Persians conquer Babylonia. Some Judahites resettle in Judah.
450	Jerusalem becomes capital of Judah with new temple. New Samarian temple built in Gerizim.
333	Defeat of Persia by Alexander of Macedon.
323–198	Ptolemies of Egypt rule Palestine.
198	Seleucids of Syria take control of Palestine.
140	After successful revolt, Hasmoneans rule over Judah/Judea.
63–	Incorporation of Palestine into the Roman Empire.

Timeline of ancient Palestinian History

HISTORY AND ARCHAEOLOGY

Before archaeological investigation properly began in Palestine in the nineteenth century, the Bible provided the only source available for the pre-classical period. That story was, after all, part of Christian belief and provided its worldview. No alternative account of the past was attempted until the nineteenth century, when earlier doubts about Moses's authorship of the Law were developed into a full-scale analysis in which four major documents were identified within these five books. When separated and arranged in a chronological sequence, they provided a portrait of Israelite religion in which Law came not at the beginning but towards the end, replacing a more 'ethical' and spontaneous spirit reflected in the Prophets. Stories of Israel's early life in their land did not seem to suggest knowledge of much of the Law at all. The view that Law came to be a dominant criterion of Judaism only relatively late on has since become standard among scholars. Yet such methods and reconstructions could not be independently confirmed; they were based only on internal contradictions.

On his campaign in Egypt in 1798, Napoleon had brought along 150 scholars whose task was to explore and recover ancient Egyptian civilization. The explosion of interest that this generated sparked off a similar quest by other nations to recover the world of the Bible as well. Soon, national societies were established devoting themselves to Palestine's history. Religious interests mixed with scientific ones from the beginning, however, and these have always tried to misrepresent or subvert archaeological research. An internet search will reveal a majority of sites that simply reassert the biblical story.

In the popular understanding of archaeology, the uncovering of objects and buildings is the focus of interest. But what permits archaeology to offer the basis for a history is chronological measurement. Before the invention of radiometric methods of dating, this was achieved through stratigraphy and ceramic typology. Over time, ancient cities grew into mounds as successive layers of building (strata) accumulated. By carefully observing and interpreting the strata, an idea of the history of the site can be gained. Even where destruction and rebuilding happened suddenly (not an infrequent occurrence), separation of strata is not easy. But an important breakthrough came with a realization that the pottery found at ancient sites and in surveys demonstrated differences in design and manufacture that could be sequenced. Stratigraphy demonstrates only the chronology of a single site, but pottery types can be compared across sites so that comparative dating can be achieved. When an absolute date can be established at one or a few sites (a datable military campaign, an earthquake, an inscription), other sites can be aligned through their pottery. A regional history becomes possible. Radiometric measurements of vegetable and mineral materials are now directly providing absolute figures (within a certain margin) that partly overcome subjective differences in interpretations of pottery.

Archaeological research has accelerated to the point where historical scenarios are being rapidly developed at a rate that non-specialists can hardly follow. Major disagreements exist, but some consensus is emerging, and the Bible's own history can now be replaced by hard evidence. Biblical periodizations still found in popular usage ('the age of the Patriarchs', 'the reign of David', 'the period of the Judges', for instance) are disappearing from scholarly discussion. The periodization recognizable by archaeologists is as follows (though there are slight disagreements):

Bronze Age

Early Bronze (I–IV)	3330–2200 BCE
Middle Bronze (I–II)	2200–1550 BCE
Late Bronze (I–II)	1550–1200 BCE

Iron Age

Iron I	1200–920 BCE
Iron IIa	1000–925/920 BCE
Iron IIb	925–586 BCE
Iron III	586–539 BCE

Persian-Hellenistic Period
539–63 BCE

Roman Period
63 BCE–330 CE

The periods directly relevant to the Old Testament are the Iron Age and the Persian-Hellenistic period. Although the *setting* of biblical stories about Israel's earliest ancestors would have to be assigned to earlier periods, there is no useful archaeological evidence bearing on these stories, and despite odd data such as Egyptian store cities or social customs being used to support the 'historicity' of the Bible, no reliable historical setting can be identified. Archaeology works with material remains, and as far as Israel and Judah are concerned, historical traces are confined to Palestine.

During the twentieth century, interest in 'archaeology and the Bible' was in the spotlight. But the scholarly issue was not between 'text' and 'spade', but about how to read the Bible. Many advocates of archaeology thought critical dissection of the text unnecessary (and even disrespectful). But archaeology was unable to keep verifying the story. The military conquest of Canaan, in particular, became less and less probable. Neither Jericho nor Ai were destroyed when they were supposed to have been. It was also too often forgotten that the biblical story was not unanimous: the piecemeal settlement depicted in Judges fitted the archaeological picture much better than Joshua's exploits.

The final breakthrough occurred, ironically, as an outcome of the Six Day War in 1967, when Israel captured and occupied the West Bank, the region of Israel and Judah in the first millennium BCE. Israeli archaeologists conducted a survey of the occupation history of the Iron Age in this area. Survey is a vital technique: by scanning terrain for traces of habitation (often with the assistance of aerial reconnaissance), deductions about past settlement can be made. The majority of ancient populations did not live in cities, after all, but in villages or farmsteads. The results of the West Bank Survey were publicized by Israel Finkelstein in 1988, and the results have affected three historical issues in particular: the settlement of Israelites in Canaan, the kingdom of David and Solomon, and the 'return' from Babylonian exile. Arising from these reconstructions is also the definition of 'Israel' itself.

We can concentrate on these three issues as a way to understand the Bible's stories. As explained in the previous chapter, historical accuracy or inaccuracy is not—*and could not be*—the point of these stories. Sometimes they happen to be reliable, sometimes not. Inscriptions of foreign rulers mention Israel, Judah, some individual kings and historical events. The destruction of Samaria in 722, and the deportation of Judahites to Babylon by Nebuchadnezzar in 596 and 586 are both recorded by the victorious kings, while Nebuchadnezzar's transfer of government from Jerusalem to Mizpah is supported by surveys of the population distribution of that period.

THE 'ISRAELITE SETTLEMENT'

The West Bank survey of early Iron Age settlement (1250–1050 BCE) showed that, as the previous political and economic structure of city-states weakened, new villages began to appear in the highlands. These began in the northern central highlands (what became the kingdom of Israel) and, as has become increasingly clear, appeared only later in the more southerly hills of Judah. No military conquest seems to have been involved in the initial settlement, and the material culture (pottery, architecture, diet) does not betray any hint of foreign origin: the villagers were locals. These findings obviously challenge the biblical story of a nation arriving from Egypt and taking over the land by force. Two major consequences of this are that archaeology must write its history independent of the Old Testament, and that the biblical stories from Genesis to Joshua cannot be explained on the whole as 'Israelite folk memory' or 'Israelite tradition'.

Settlement in Judah was first understood as an expansion of the process to the north, so that all the settlers could see themselves as a single society. But subsequent analysis shows that the two regions developed separately, and at different rates, with Judah remaining well behind in population growth, economic activity, and thus political development. It is now that the two kingdoms that later emerged in Israel and Judah arose independently. The biblical portrait in 1 Samuel of two 'houses' of Israel and Judah actually supports this. But the sequel, a united kingdom based in Jerusalem, is more problematic, and an 'empire' of extended territory can definitely be ruled out. What, then, can the historian write about the monarchic period?

THE BEGINNINGS OF MONARCHY: DAVID AND SOLOMON

Israelite monarchy is popularly associated with David and Solomon. According to the books of Samuel, the Israelites asked for a king, and chose one. But the emergence of a monarchy is a gradual process. It develops out of a system of patronage. Certain families and individuals become more wealthy and powerful, and are able to offer protection to other families in return for some form of payment. These individuals may originally come from inside or outside. Such a client retains power through retainers loyal to him personally. The history of some recently independent states shows how quickly and easily leaders can assume total control, once they have acquired a critical mass of loyal followers. Our modern concept of 'king' is too precise for the Hebrew word *melek*, which might designate anyone from a city mayor to the ruler of an empire. But the existence of a 'king' points to a politically organized and stratified society marked archaeologically by evidence of a certain level of economic activity, population density, urbanization, monumental architecture, craft specialization and luxury goods.

These features define what archaeologists identify as Iron II. The kingdoms of Israel and Judah were not simply a natural expansion of the highland villages but incorporated many of the cities that existed alongside them, as well as newly-built ones. But when was this stage reached? Three alternative chronologies have been offered for the beginning of Iron II. The conventional date, accepted until quite recently, was 1000 BCE, now referred to as the 'high chronology'. A 'low chronology', proposed by Israel Finkelstein, places the date at about 925, while a 'modified conventional chronology', favoured by Amihai Mazar, fits halfway between them (see the table below). Fifty years or so may not seem a great time difference, but it is crucial because this gap falls around the period that would be assigned to the reign of David.

Conventional chronology	Low chronology	Modified conventional chronology
Iron Ia 1200–1140/30	1200–1140/30	1200–1140/30
Iron Ib 1150–1000	1130–920/900	1140/30–980
Iron IIa 1000–900/925	920/900–800/780	980–830
Iron IIb 900/925–732/700	780–732/701	830–732/701

Chronologies for the origins of monarchy

The 'high' chronology was initially achieved by working back from the reigns of monarchs in the books of Kings, and the date of 1000 BCE aligned with David's defeat of the Philistines and the extension of his rule over most, if not all, of the land (again, following biblical data). Archaeological data initially appeared to support this calculation. Philistine pottery ceased in central Palestine (because David had repelled them), while monumental buildings in central-northern cities suggested a great building programme, such as the one attributed to Solomon in the books of Kings. The city gates of Hazor, Gezer and Megiddo all had towers and six chambers inside the entryway, set into heavy casemate walls, suggesting one powerful king responsible for all three. And 1 Kings 9:15 mentions Solomon as having built (or rebuilt) these three cities. But new sites and re-excavations bring new data and new calculations, and the activity attributed to Solomon at Megiddo now seems more likely to belong to Ahab, who was king of Israel a century later.

The archaeology of Jerusalem is also crucial. The books of Samuel state that David captured and rebuilt the city. But while there is plenty of pottery here from earlier and later periods, not much has turned up for Iron I or IIa. Estimates of Jerusalem's status at this time range from a small unfortified village to a major capital city. But of monumental buildings there is little trace. One feature has become a focus of attention, a 'stepped stone structure' at the edge of the hill on which the Iron-Age city was located. A building above this structure has been claimed by some archaeologists for David, while others have concluded that it is not even a single building and that parts of it may be 600 years or more later. Such a discrepancy is a reminder of just how open to interpretation archaeology can sometimes be, and how fraught with religious and nationalistic interests. On a sober assessment, Jerusalem's archaeological record, which has been quite extensively explored, does not fit the capital city of an extensive kingdom. This does not mean that a David never existed, but that his biblical profile is questionable.

One further aspect of the debate about the early monarchy is a campaign of the Egyptian pharaoh, Sheshonq, whose reign began in 945 or 943 BCE, and whom 1 Kings 11:40 dates to the reign of Solomon and his successor Rehoboam. Sheshonq left a stele in Egypt on which he claimed to have conquered 180 places in Palestine. According to 1 Kings 14:25 and 2 Chronicles 12:1-12, 'Shishak' plundered Jerusalem. Almost inevitably, it was concluded that this is what brought an end to Solomon's empire. But the pharaoh does not include Jerusalem in his extensive list of cities, though he did campaign in the area of Benjamin just to the north. This might rather suggest he was targeting a kingdom such as Saul's, which would fit the 'low chronology'.

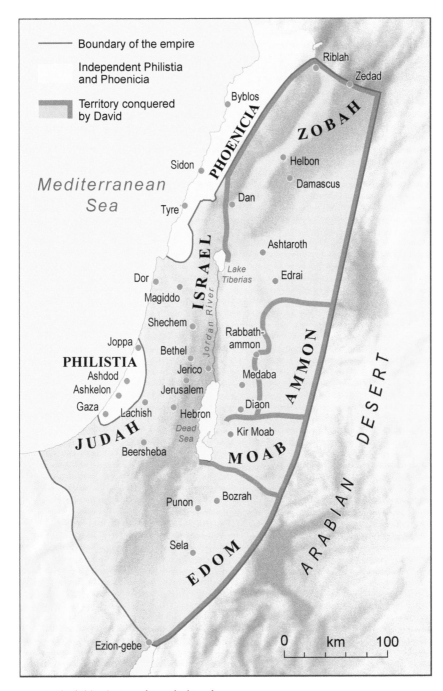

Map 2: The biblical view of David's kingdom

The 'high chronology' has now more or less been abandoned, and the 'modified' and 'low' chronologies are battling it out. Radiometry seems to be on the side of the 'low' chronology, but the methods are not as straight-forward as they might seem. The margin of error of a single radiocarbon reading may lie across the tenth and the ninth centuries BCE, so that a large number of readings is necessary. But victory for the 'low chronology' would all but remove the kingdoms of David and Solomon from history, and assign the beginning of a stable monarchy to the economically more advanced northern highlands of Israel, where the kingdom was known to others as the 'house of Omri'. Whether an earlier kingdom under Saul, centred in Benjamin (just north of Jerusalem), preceded it cannot be con-firmed, but any remains in Jerusalem from this time might be his rather than David's. As things stand, David and Solomon have left no unquestion-able archaeological trace.

The name 'Israel'

The form of this is a verb followed by the word for 'god' (*el*), resembling many personal names: in Genesis 32:28, Jacob is told 'You shall no longer be called Jacob, but Israel'. But this story is much more probably the result of an attempt to establish Jacob as the ancestor of the people of a kingdom already known as Israel. 'Israel' may, however, have been a tribal name. The earliest established reference to people called 'Israel' dates from the end of the thirteenth century BCE, from the Egyptian king, Merneptah, celebrating a successful military campaign:

> The princes lie prostrate, saying 'peace'
> None raises his head among the Nine Bows
> Tehenu destroyed, Hatti pacified
> Canaan is plundered with every misery
> Ashkelon is taken, Gezer is captured
> Yanoam has been made non-existent
> Israel lies desolate; its seed is no more
> Hurru has become a widow for To-meri [Egypt]
> All lands together have become peaceful
> Everyone who was a nomad has been reined in by king...Merneptah

Merneptah's Israel lies somewhere in Palestine, and 'Israel' is marked with a sign that identifies it with a rural (agricultural or nomadic) population, not a place. It is possible, even likely, that the 'Israel' of this inscription refers to some or to all of the people recently established in the highlands. But the name itself does not necessarily transmit a fixed identity. We cannot eas-ily equate the earliest Israel (if correctly identified) with any of the biblical Israels. We have a name in continuous use, but cannot assign it to a fixed ethnic population.

THE KINGDOM OF ISRAEL

Three centuries after Merneptah's stele and the emergence of highland villages, a kingdom called 'Israel' appears. We can deduce the processes that led from one to the other. The village populations integrated through intermarriage and economic cooperation, but also interacted with urban populations. Did the subjects of the kingdom all identify themselves as 'Israelites' and if so, what did this mean to them? More likely, they identified with their village or tribe. Their religious practices and beliefs, for example, do not seem to have been distinctive, nor their customs. When the inhabitants of the city of Dan were conquered by Aram, did they remain 'Israelite' or become 'Aramean'? We can be sure they remained 'Danite' and spoke not Hebrew, or Aramaic, but the dialect of Dan.

Evidence of the Israelite kingdom comes from inscriptions, mostly of the Assyrian kings who threatened both Israel and Aram, forcing them sometimes into combined resistance. Shalmaneser III (859–842 BCE) records how he fought (in 853) a battle at Qarqar in Syria against a coalition led by Hadadezer of Aram and including 'Ahab the Israelite'. But 'Israel' is not the usual name for the kingdom itself. The Assyrians preferred 'house of Omri' or 'Samaria', the ruling house or the capital. Shalmaneser also records a campaign a decade later against these same kingdoms and includes, in relief, Jehu 'son of Omri' doing obeisance. Adad-nirari III (809–783) claims to have mastered all of Syria and Palestine and to have received tribute from 'Joash the Samarian'. Nearly a century later, Sargon II's annals record:

> the town of the Samarians I besieged, conquered ... [for the god...] who let me achieve this my triumph... I led away as prisoners [27,290 inhabitants of it (and) equipped from among them (soldiers to man)] 50 chariots for my royal corps... The town I rebuilt better than it was before and settled there people from countries which I had conquered.

Whether the details in these inscriptions are accurate is another matter, of course. Military reports are always suspect!

JUDAH AND THE 'HOUSE OF DAVID'

There is another inscriptional reference to the 'house of Omri'/'Israel' to be considered. But it has more implications for Judah. An event that Assyrian and biblical sources both mention occurred after the end of the kingdom of Israel, and constitutes the first Assyrian reference to Judah, then an

Assyrian vassal. In response to the withholding of tribute, Sennacherib invaded Judah, took Lachish and other cities, besieged Jerusalem and finally withdrew. The Assyrian version, including the reliefs of the siege of Lachish from Sennacherib's palace, naturally focuses on glorifying Assyria and its king, and assumes a totally successful campaign. For the biblical accounts in 2 Kings 18–19 and Isaiah 36–39, the focus is rather on what is seen as a miraculous rescue for Jerusalem, even though it is conceded that Hezekiah had to pay a large sum of money to Sennacherib.

Earlier references to Judah, however, are missing. A different name is used. The Moabite king, Mesha, in about 840 BCE, celebrates his deliverance of Moab from Israelite domination, using the names 'Israel' and 'Omri'. But he also makes a probable reference to a 'house of David' that he also attacked. A 'house of David' occurs also in an inscription from Dan, which the Aramean king captured from Israel. The biblical version of the war with Mesha in 2 Kings 3 names a king of Israel (Jehoram) and a king of Judah (Jehoshaphat) and incidentally does not confirm Mesha's success in so many words, but ends in a curious way.

The subjugation of Judah to Israel (when not to Aram) is more than hinted at in the books of Kings. Athaliah, the daughter of King Ahab of Israel and his notorious queen Jezebel, was married to the Judahite ruler Jehoram and became the mother of Jehoram's successor, Ahaziah. Curiously, Ahab's son and successor is called Joram, which is Jehoram spelled differently. The story in 2 Kings 9–11 (which includes a coup and the murder of two kings) may conceal either a formal, if temporary annexation of Judah to Israel, or a 'united monarchy' with Samaria in control.

What these references show is not just that Judah is never referred to as being 'Israel' or part of 'Israel', but is not called 'Judah' either. While the kingdom of Israel took its name—apparently—from a population group, Judah was the name of the land. Its population apparently comprised several tribal groups (Caleb, Kenaz and Simeon are mentioned in Genesis and Judges). The 'tribe of Judah' seems to be a biblical fiction. The rulers of this land are the 'house of David', which becomes the 'kingdom of Judah', but when? As mentioned earlier, the title 'king' is flexible and the ruler from the 'house of David' possibly called himself a 'king'. But apparently no-one else did until Judah came under Assyrian hegemony.

It is often claimed that the two references to the 'house of David' prove David's historical existence. This is a not unexpected optimistic reaction. The expression 'house of Omri' does suggest a historical Omri (biblical texts mention him briefly) and 'Omri' is a well-known personal name; 'David' is not a personal name, and may be a nickname or a title. But the house itself

Figure 3: Detail from Sennacherib's relief of the siege of Lachish (British Museum)

had an origin and a founder. Within Judah, 'David' was taken as a personal name and inspired a number of stories, many clearly legendary. It is one thing to say there may have been a 'David' but quite another to claim that the biblical character is real.

We have gone as far as we can with the historicity of David, Solomon, his successor Rehoboam, and Jeroboam, the major characters in the creation and dissolution of the 'Davidic kingdom'. But this epoch seems to have much to do with the relationship between the 'Israels' identified in the previous chapter: of the Mosaic books (12 tribes, including a tribe of Judah), the kingdom of Israel based in Samaria (Kings), and the Israel consisting only of Judahites (as in Ezra and Nehemiah and possibly implied in Kings). These 'Israels' cannot simply be conflated and the historian must somehow deal with them. But the answer lies within the biblical stories even more than with archaeology.

THE PROVINCES OF JUDAH AND SAMARIA AND THE 'RETURN'

Now we pick up the third of the issues identified earlier as the focus of this chapter. The history of the province of Samaria, as we have seen, is treated briefly and polemically in the Old Testament. According to the New Testament too, Jews do not share with Samari(t)ans (John 4:9) and treat them like Gentiles (Matthew 10:5). Evidently, enmity developed between them at some point and 'Samaritans' has remained a pejorative term for what came to be regarded as a fringe sect. Samarians share the Mosaic canon with Jews, implying a time when both societies enjoyed fraternal relations and agreeing upon a common history. References both inside and outside the Old Testament point to intermarriage between the priesthoods of Jerusalem and the Samarian temple of Gerizim that was (re)built about the same time as Jerusalem, in the fifth century. When hostility crept in is uncertain: scholars currently suggest only after Alexander's conquests in the late third century.

As remarked in the previous chapter, not a great deal is said in the Old Testament about Judah between the end of the kingdom and the return of Judahites from Babylonia and the rebuilding of Jerusalem's city and temple. But the 'Return' is a major ingredient in the definition of 'Israel' as Judah. The Babylonian Chronicles offer a reasonably sober and reliable record of Nebuchadnezzar's two deportations from Judah (597 and 586), the second accompanied by the sacking of Jerusalem. The numbers of deportees vary even among the biblical sources (Kings and Jeremiah), but clearly a substantial segment was removed, particularly from the Jerusalem region. A policy of 'regime change' saw power transferred to Benjaminite leaders.

Survey data reveal an initial depopulation of the Jerusalem area, with a slight increase in Benjamin. This is reversed during the fifth century, but slowly. The change of capital and regime meant the possibility of a change of relations between Judah and Samaria, if the new regime in Judah was less hostile than Jerusalem's elite had been. It also meant a cult other than that of the god of Jerusalem. Which temples and which priestly lines now dominated? And what happened when these arrangements were brought to an end as the Persians reinstated Jerusalem? We might well imagine resentment growing between Judahites loyal to their old rulers and Benjaminites, as well as between Samarians, regarding themselves as the real 'house of Israel' and the new Judahite 'Israel' that returned. The persistent antagonism in the Old Testament towards the kingdom of Israel and the Samarians, and the struggle between Saul of Benjamin and David of Judah have a very plausible context in these conflicting interests, and in the period when we can see two provincial 'Israels' competing against each other, and against a third that brought them together.

The biblical narrative tells how an ethnic Israel becomes a political Israel. Historically, the reverse is more probable: an originally political Israel became an ethnic Israel as Judah was included. How could this occur? Hardly before the fall of the Judahite monarchy, whose kings would not have wished to be associated with the Assyrian province of Samaria. But Benjamin's affinity with Samaria was closer. In the maternal code of Genesis, Jacob's favourite wife, Rachel, bears Joseph and Benjamin (Joseph is represented by the two major tribes of Israel, Ephraim and Manasseh). Another factor is Bethel, the site of an Israelite temple, which was at some point incorporated into Judah and thus almost certainly belonged to Benjamin. If it replaced Jerusalem as the major sanctuary, it could serve both provinces, uniting them under the protection of the god of Israel/Jacob, and embracing Judah as a son. This hypothesis is hard to prove but it explains the twelve-tribe Israel, while the politics of the era explain the subsequent antagonism between Samaria, Benjamin and Judah that dominate the historical and prophetic books of the Old Testament.

Part Three

Stories of Jesus Christ

Chapter Six

Ancient Judaisms

We have seen how 'Israel' is an identity with several claimants, each with its own story. In the case of the New Testament, we have a multiplicity of 'Jesuses'. There is more than one memory of a historical figure and more than one understanding of what followers of Jesus Christ, as he becomes, should believe and do. The New Testament exposes these identities, ending in a highly vivid climax: Jesus Christ returns to defeat his enemies, gather the righteous to himself and bring creation and history to an end.

The stories begin in Palestine with a Jewish teacher and healer understood by his followers as the culmination of all that the scriptures mean. They move beyond Palestine and beyond Judaism, and what begins as a confrontation with Jewish authorities ends as a confrontation with the Roman Empire. But they give only hints of the eventful history of their time and little explanation of the culture of first century CE Palestinian Judaism. The original readers, of course, did not need telling, but two thousand years later, some explanation is necessary.

POLITICS

Alexander's conquest of the Persian Empire (beginning in 334) generated a fusion of Greek and Near Eastern culture that is called 'Hellenism' and, as far as Judah was involved, two kingdoms centred in Alexandria and Antioch, named, after their founding generals, Ptolemaic and Seleucid. Judah was affected by the cultural change, which brought it first under Ptolemaic (312–198), the Seleucid rule. Among the large Jewish population in the newly-built city of Alexandria, the Greek language and ideas were creatively fused with Jewish customs and beliefs. Alexandria was, however, only one of many cities of the Roman Empire in which Jewish populations grew. Their various Judaisms focused on Judah as the ethnic homeland and involved pilgrimage and temple taxes, but they also adapted in different degrees to the surrounding culture, including its literature, religious iconography and philosophy.

Political history receives only sporadic attention in the New Testament but it has an important bearing on the rise of Christianity. Casting a shadow over Judah's history is the Hasmonean kingdom, which, after four hundred years, revived political aspirations. This kingdom was built on a successful revolt in 167 against the Seleucid king, Antiochus III, under whom Jerusalem was converted into a city after the Greek model, with institutions such as a gymnasium, council, baths, schools and, of course, cults.

Such measures were welcomed by the people of Samaria, which was renamed Sebaste, and in Jerusalem there was some local support, but a revolt was sparked off by the replacement of the existing cult and ban on core Jewish customs. After military successes by the Jews under Judas the 'Maccabee' and his brothers, the temple was rededicated and semi-autonomy granted, leading to full independence. Assuming at first the high priesthood, the rulers then assumed the title of king as well.

The Hasmoneans could claim no Davidic descent, nor did they belong to the high-priestly lineages. Rivalries that had contributed to Antiochus's measures persisted. Internal division is a common outcome of newly-won independence, and with political, religious and economic power closer to home, pressure groups engaged with the native rulers. The historian Josephus describes how the Pharisees and Sadducees vied for influence.

The Hasmonean kingdom had, nevertheless, expanded into most of Palestine. The Samaritan temple of Gerizim, near Shechem, was destroyed in this process. Modern historians often speak of 'forcible conversion' of the conquered population to Judaism. But most already practised circumcision (never a unique Jewish custom), and even worshipped a high god. This was the case with Samarians and possibly with Idumeans (ancient Edom) who occupied territory once belonging to Judah. The main effect of Judah's political enlargement was the dominance of the Jerusalem temple, and the production of a Palestine-wide 'Judaism'. (It is ironic that from the conquered regions of Galilee and Idumaea came, respectively, Jesus and Herod the Great.)

Despite their nationalistic credentials, the Hasmoneans were quite Hellenistic in their way of life. Civil unrest was never far away and the two sons of the Hasmonean queen, Salome (Shelomzion), fell out with one another, with the Pharisees supporting one (Hyrcanus) and the Sadducees the other (Aristobulus—note the Greek names). The impasse was resolved by the Roman general Pompey, initially welcomed by all sides, who

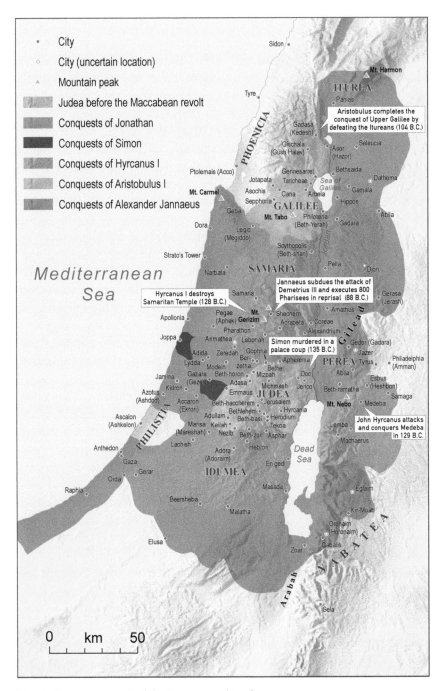

Map 3: The enlargement of the Hasmonean kingdom

entered Jerusalem in 64 BCE, leaving Hyrcanus as a puppet king and taking Aristobulus to Rome.

During the Roman civil war between Pompey and Caesar, Antipater supported Caesar and sent forces to relieve him in Alexandria, as a result of which Jews were to be favoured as members of a 'lawful religion' and exempted from certain taxes. Caesar left Antipater as procurator of Judea, and Antipater appointed his sons over Galilee (Herod) and over Jerusalem (Phasael). Aristobulus invaded with the help of the Parthians, whose empire now stretched from eastern Iran as far west as the Jordan. Phasael was killed and the Parthians occupied Jerusalem. With Roman help, Herod recaptured Judea and was appointed 'king of the Jews' by the Roman senate.

As a ruler, Herod was effective and achieved much for his subjects. As 'king of the Jews', his patronage extended to Jewish communities outside Judea. Herod's kingdom was, in most respects, a continuation of the Hasmonean kingdom, as Herod himself wished it to appear by marrying a Hasmonean princess. But Herod did not claim the high priesthood (though he appointed his own candidates for that office). He was arguably the greatest builder of his generation, founding, among other projects, the city of Tiberias and the port of Caesarea, and reconstructing the Jerusalem temple.

He did not, incidentally, order the massacre of any children. That story, in Matthew's Gospel, aims to parallel the story of Moses's birth in Exodus. But, despite political ability and personal charm, Herod was unpopular with many of the populace. He was paranoid and had a number of family members (including two sons and his Hasmonean wife, Mariamne) killed. Before he died from some unpleasant disease in 4 BCE, Herod proposed dividing his kingdom between his sons, and since the family also took the name of 'Herod', it is easy to confuse the various rulers (as the gospel writers did). In 6 CE, a Roman province of Judea was formed, incorporating Samaria and Idumea, while Philip ruled the northerly territories of Batanea, Trachonitis and Auranitis. In 34 BCE, these were incorporated into Syria, then given to Herod Agrippa I, who also later took over Galilee and in 41 CE became king of Judea, though without any real power. The details of this patchwork are actually even more complicated and take no account of the independent Greek cities like the Decapolis. What had been a single Jewish kingdom at the death of Herod became, during the lifetime of Jesus, a political patchwork.

RELIGION

Within Judea, the Pharisees and Sadducees may have retained their political interests but increasingly developed into religious parties,

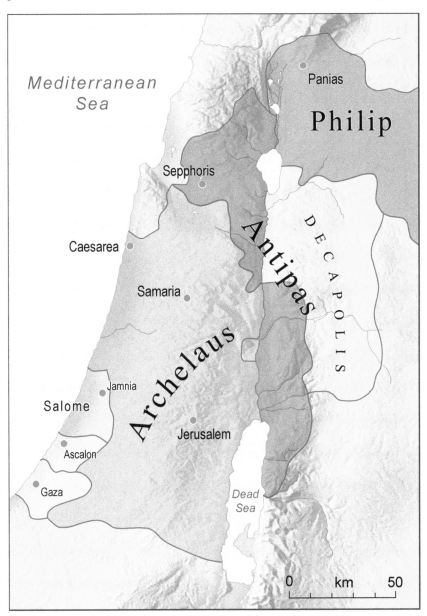

Map 4: The division of Herod the Great's kingdom among his sons after his death

whose beliefs and practices, along with a third party, the Essenes, will be described below. A fourth group grew out of a nationalistic party led by Judah the Galilean, which initiated a rebellion against the Romans in 6 CE, when Quirinius came into Judea (this official is placed by Luke at the birth of Jesus). The uprising, mentioned in Acts 5:37, was quashed, but its activists persisted. During the first Jewish revolt of 66, Josephus reports bands of *sicarii*, or 'knifers' at large. It has been common to group these activists under the name of 'Zealots', but the term may indicate a revolutionary disposition rather than a party. The name of the disciple of Jesus, Judas Iscariot, might be a corruption of 'Judah the Sicari'; and 'Simon the

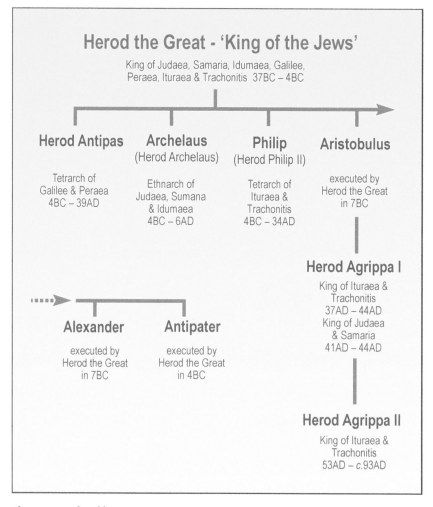

Chart 2: Herod and his successors

Zealot' is mentioned in Luke 6:15 and Acts 1:13. These names have raised the suspicion that Jesus's followers contained people associated with violent resistance to Roman rule.

Political unrest in the story of Jesus's life is hardly visible, though it can be detected. The gospel stories have a limited focus: disciples, religious authorities, crowds. Roman intervention is confined to the judgment and execution—and is benignly reported. This last factor may be due to the writers' unwillingness to hint at anything that might seem like insurrection against Rome, which would not appeal to many would-be converts, including diaspora Jews.

JEWISH BELIEFS AND PRACTICES

The religious differences in this period justify the use of the plural 'Judaisms'. 'Judaism' itself was the kind of ethnic marker that multicultural empires, from the Assyrian onwards, recognized as a necessary extension of national or provincial identities based on geography. These ethnic labels covered a range of cultural variations among diasporas, but basic cultural features persisted, sustained by stories, customs and religious practices, and a common 'homeland', especially Jerusalem and its temple. But differences existed about what Jews should believe, how they should behave—and how the temple should function.

For many outsiders, Judaism was a 'philosophy'—that is, what we would now call a religion, defined by belief in its one god. For the Romans and Greeks, religion was not exclusive and was rather a matter of practice, of cultic celebration, especially sacrifices. To Romans or Greeks, religion did not define which god they worshipped, because they worshipped several. Jews would have stood out by not performing sacrifices, but instead observing sabbaths and festivals, assembling in synagogues and observing some quaint dietary rules. Living outside Judah, they were not subject to the scriptural laws about agriculture, but the Law was read systematically at Sabbath gatherings. Like most minority ethnic groups, Jews tended to inhabit their own quarters in the large cities. How far they restricted social contact with non-Jews is hard to know and was probably variable.

Greek philosophical ideas were engaged by educated Jews. Allegorical interpretation of the Law, adopted from Stoicism, was used by Philo of Alexandria. Greek belief in a soul did not fit well with Jewish belief in resurrection but in various ways this was accommodated (Paul made his own effort). Magic and astrology were not universally avoided, either. Zodiacs have been found on synagogue floors (even in Palestine), and images of biblical figures modeled on classical heroes (David as Orpheus, for example) and Jewish bowls with magic incantations have been widely found. However we imagine Jewish communities in the Roman Empire, they were not generally reclusive, nor suspicious or resentful of non-Jewish culture, but one of many ethnicities in the cosmopolitan Greek-Roman world— and in what we now call the Middle East, too, though the New Testament ignores them.

Jews had little reason to embrace the teachings of the Christian apostles. For one thing, outside Palestine, most were not interested in liberation from Rome and certainly not in a deliverer with no military credentials or agenda. As for deliverance from sin and death, Judaism itself provided for this and Jews would not abandon their devotion to God's law, however little some may have observed it. There were those who embraced both Jesus Christ and Judaism, but these lie outside the New Testament orbit, other than as vilified 'Judaizers'.

But while the New Testament came into being within the Roman world, and in Greek, the story of Jesus is set in Palestine. Here, we can take just the better-known varieties of Judaism, while being aware that everyday Jewish belief was no doubt much more variegated.

Figure 4: Zodiac mosaic floor of the Bet Alpha synagogue (sixth century CE)

THE DEAD SEA SCROLLS

The discovery in 1947 of (mostly) Hebrew manuscripts stored in caves beside a settlement on the western Dead Sea shore known as Qumran includes writings composed during the lifetime of Jesus. They are the most direct evidence of what some of his contemporaries believed and did. But how typical is this collection? Is it from the library of a sect, such as the Essenes, who are mentioned by several ancient writers, or were these writings rescued from various Jewish libraries as the Romans closed in on Jerusalem during the first Jewish revolt? There is no agreement among scholars over why these scrolls came to be in the caves, nor who preserved them. No one religious profile can be traced from these manuscripts, though there are many common features that point to a distinct strand (or strands) of Jewish belief and behaviour.

The remains of over 900 scrolls have been identified, and 300 different compositions, so most of the writings are preserved in more than one manuscript. The compositions fall into three categories. The largest of these is scriptural: all writings of the Hebrew canon are found, except Esther and possibly Ezra and Nehemiah in their canonical form. The variety of textual forms, however, shows that no one edition had yet been canonized among the owners. The second category is of Jewish writings already known to us, in particular 1 Enoch and Jubilees, previously preserved only in Ethiopic but now available (in fragments) in their original languages of Aramaic and Hebrew respectively. The third category is of texts previously unknown, including those often described as 'sectarian' since several describe segregated communities. Possibly one or more of these once occupied Qumran, a settlement close to the scroll caves which was excavated initially during the 1950s and again in recent years. It was judged to have been inhabited between about 100 BCE and 68 CE.

THE CALENDAR AND THE ORIGIN OF EVIL

Several Qumran texts (along with 1 Enoch and Jubilees) reflect the observance of a 364-day calendar divided into exactly 52 weeks. The calendar followed in the Jerusalem cult was of twelve lunar months. Both calendars, of course, needed adjusting to the true solar year. The lunar calendar, about 10 days short of the solar year, was (and still is) adjusted by inserting an extra month before the spring equinox when a thirteenth new moon appeared since the last equinox; the solar calendar provided twelve months independent of the lunar cycle and comprising 30 days each, with (according to some texts at least) four 'quarter days'. How further adjustment was made we do not know. The adherents of each calendar would regard the others as offending God by performing his required festivals wrongly. But the underlying problem is the incompatibility of sun and moon. The agricultural year depends on the sun and the seasons. But weeks (and hence Sabbaths) depend on the moon. The Old Testament supports both sides, and neither. It generally reflects the lunar calendar, but within the Flood story (Genesis 6–9) are 30-day months.

The theological problem was that God had created both sun and moon. How could their discrepancy be explained? It is explained in 1 Enoch by a revolt in heaven that led to disorder there as well as on earth, where the rebel angels mixed with humans to create a race of giants who were killed off in the Flood. Sin therefore did not originate with humans, but with these angels and the evil spirits who emanated from them. The leader of the rebels was imprisoned by God in the wilderness but remained a threat to humans (tempting Jesus, for example). There are hints of this myth in the Old Testament, in a story of fallen angels in Genesis 6:1-4, and the ceremony of the Day of Atonement (Leviticus 16), where Israel's sins are placed on a goat and sent off back 'to Azazel', one of the names of the angelic leader.

Genesis offers another myth about the origin of sin, in which Adam disobeyed a divine command and all his descendants were punished. But there remained also a belief in a supernatural evil Satanic figure, hence the Day of Atonement ceremony. Both Judaism and Christianity have maintained this dual explanation: Satan tempts, humans sin. The snake in the Garden of Eden has been transformed into Satan, despite the explicit comment that the snake was a creature made by God. According to Jewish law, however, sins can be atoned for by repentance and appropriate cultic action, such as washing and sacrifice. But the Christian gospel, as fashioned by Paul, teaches that sinful humans are doomed unless they are perfect, which is impossible. Only Jesus's death can remove the law's punishment for human sin and thereby free humans from sin and Adam's punishment of death.

We can finish off this topic by returning to the sun and the moon. The writers of Genesis 1 cleverly avoid this controversy: neither controls the calendar!

And God said, 'Let there be lights in the dome of the sky to separate the day from the night; and let them be for signs and for seasons and for days and years, and let them be lights in the dome of the sky to give light upon the earth'. And it was so. God made the two great lights—the greater light to rule the day and the lesser light to rule the night—and the stars.

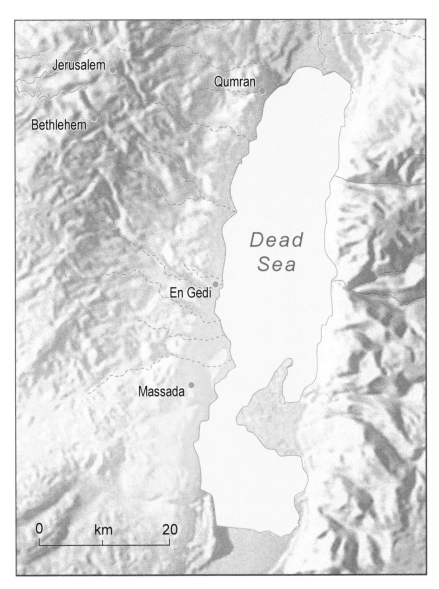

Map 5: The location of Qumran

Figure 5: Site of Qumran settlement with Cave 4

The Qumran manuscripts place the Mosaic law at the centre of community life, but they also give prominence to evil as a cosmic principle. Like
1 Enoch, they relate the fall of the rebellious angels (called the 'Watchers')
and identify an evil archangel with various names (Melchiresha, Prince of
Darkness, Mastema, Belial), even embracing a dualistic view of the universe like Zoroastrianism—the religion of the Parthians. One text describes
a final war of Light versus Darkness. Dualistic beliefs have persisted on the
fringes of both Judaism and Christianity ever since.

There has been speculation that either John the Baptist or Jesus, or
both, had some contact with the communities described in the scrolls of
the Dead Sea. There are some similarities, but the range of beliefs among
the Judaisms of Jesus's time was wide, and shared features need to be cau-
tiously interpreted.

1 ENOCH AND JUBILEES

Both of these books can be described as 'apocalyptic' (see Chapter 12), in
claiming to be revelations about the future. Several books were attributed
to Enoch, but only 1 Enoch is relevant here. It is a compilation of Aramaic
writings dating from the third century BCE to perhaps the first century CE.

Enoch appears in Genesis 5, where he is mysteriously said to have 'walked with God, and was not, for God took him'. He also lived 365 years, hinting at Enoch's connection with a solar calendar. Apart from the story of the origin of sin, already covered, it contains an astronomical section (linked to its solar calendar) and a feature shared with other Jewish writings of the time—a division of world history into periods, according to a divine plan. Such histories are meant to show that the world will soon reach its allotted end. In Daniel, these are multiples of 'weeks of years'. So many of these are prescribed, then history will end. The book of Daniel contains a number of these. Interestingly, while some calendars begin with the creation of the world, others go back only to the 'Exile', and suggest that the centuries since this event are in fact a prolongation of this exile.

Jubilees, which calls itself the 'Book of the division of days', claims to be an angelic revelation on Sinai, rehearsing the story in Genesis. Even before the Law was revealed, claims the writer, the Israelite ancestors, from Abraham onwards, had followed it, along with a solar calendar. The occasion for its writing may be the Hasmonean conquests, bringing many more Jews who perhaps claimed Abraham as their forefather but did not necessarily respect Moses and the law. Like Enoch, Jubilees divides its history into 'weeks of years'—a 'jubilee' being 49 or 50. Enoch, the Dead Sea Scrolls and Jubilees demonstrate that alongside a Judaism based on strict observance of the Mosaic Law, there could be expectations of the end of the world, which scholars call 'apocalyptic'.

RABBINIC JUDAISM

After the destruction of the Jerusalem temple, a form of Judaism developed by the rabbis became the norm—though only gradually. Rabbinic Judaism can plausibly be seen as an extension of the Pharisaic agenda of interpreting and explaining how exactly the law should be faithfully fulfilled, and its rulings are attributed to several generations of rabbis, including some from the time of Jesus. The 'scribes' that figure among Jesus's opponents would have been experts in interpretation of the scriptural law. The rabbis produced a compendium of their regulations in the Mishnah (ca. 200 CE) and in the sixth-century Talmud. Whether or not rabbinic writings can be directly compared and contrasted to the New Testament, Christian scholars took rabbinic Judaism as their model for centuries, considering it a dry, legalistic system. But that is a caricature of rabbinic Judaism and ignores other varieties of early Judaism. Now that we do appreciate this variety, no longer can the gospel message be opposed to 'Judaism'; rather, it has to be carefully assessed against a spectrum of beliefs and practices.

MESSIAH

The gospels give the impression that 'the Messiah' was a figure expected by the Jews of Jesus's time and that this messiah would be a descendant of David, a kingly figure. There are two major problems with this impression. One is that messianic expectation was not common to all Jews and that various redeemer figures were being proposed. Sometimes there were two messiahs, one priestly, one lay. The Psalms of Solomon, a Jewish work from the first century, alludes to a future Davidic king, probably to replace the Hasmonean dynasty, who would overthrow the Romans. Dead Sea scrolls contain a variety of such figures: two messiahs, an angelic redeemer (Melchizedek), a 'prince', or none at all. The 'son of man' is another messianic-like figure, of whom Daniel 7:13-14 says:

> ...like a human being (literally 'son of man'), coming with the clouds of heaven. And he came to the Ancient One and was presented before him. To him was given dominion and glory and kingship, that all peoples, nations, and languages should serve him.

Jesus's use of the title in the gospels is surely intended to identify him as this humanlike but divine figure. Yet, such a figure, like the Davidic contender, is supposed to be a deliverer, not from sins but from political domination.

And here is the second problem: could Jesus be plausibly presented as any one of the commonly expected Jewish 'messiahs'? There are strong clues that he was executed as a 'king'. But his story, which we now follow, does not fulfil this ambition during his earthly life. His 'messianic' claim will rest on a second coming, where, appropriately, the New Testament will end.

Chapter Seven

The Gospels Story

The books of the Old Testament are either anonymous or pseudonymous and mostly rewritten and edited more than once. They are also varied in their interests and ideas. The New Testament books are not anonymous (with the exception of the Letter to the Hebrews), but mostly pseudonymous. They all focus on the deity Jesus Christ and were written within the space of a century. The Jewish scriptures are the work of scribal schools, finally given an official authorization (probably by the Hasmonean rulers). No scribal schools or political authorities account for the growth and canonizing of the New Testament; local Christian communities ('churches') at first adopted their own list of books, but as these communities developed into larger organizations and hierarchies emerged, culminating with the dominance of the church in Rome, the contents of the New Testament became more widely agreed.

The New Testament story contains no historiography. The Gospels and Acts are kinds of biographies; Acts, while narrating the spread of the cult of Jesus Christ throughout the Roman Empire, largely features the ministry of Saul/Paul of Tarsus. Luke's Gospel and Acts form a two-volume work, both of which aim to describe 'what Jesus did and taught' personally and then through the 'holy spirit'.

Where does the story of Jesus Christ begin? The answer is: with the Jewish scriptures. As explained in Chapter 1, the earliest Christian Bible was the Old Testament, and it was by reading the Old Testament in a certain way that the first Christians understood Jesus Christ and the apostles preached him. Despite being addressed to non-Jews, so much of the New Testament presupposes a knowledge of the Jewish scriptures. Was this because these non-Jews were already on the fringes of Judaism? Or that these scriptures were well known outside Jewish circles? No: to hear the gospel meant hearing first what the Jewish scriptures *really* meant to the believer. Otherwise, no explanation makes sense. Even so, the scriptures could be used in many ways, and many senses could be derived from them. A convenient way to see (or hear) the wealth of such interpretations is from Jennens and Handel's *Messiah*, which is very largely compiled from Old Testament texts carrying an explicit Christian story.

The foundation of the gospel, one might reasonably think, is the 'historical Jesus', which has therefore long been an obsession with New Testament scholars. But few of these adopt a strict historical methodology. A very reasonable first question from a historian might be 'Did Jesus exist?', but this has only been seriously raised in recent years and only in a few circles. A negative answer obviously leads into a cul-de-sac, but that does not make it an invalid question. It is true that other explanations of Christianity are difficult. But is that enough? A more satisfying way forward exists and was pointed out earlier in relation to biblical history. What people believe is itself a part of history, and indeed a crucial part, because beliefs about the past influence human behaviour more than whatever the facts may be. We might accept that a Jesus did exist, but there is no one 'historical Jesus' that we can confidently reconstruct. The authors of the New Testament insisted on portraying their own Jesus, while other Jesuses existed among other believers. The figure of Jesus can only be approached as a set of different images. Deciding between these images will be inconclusive, though some things can be ruled out. To make this clear, we should strictly refer only to the (shadowy) historical figure as 'Jesus', and use the title 'Jesus Christ' for the Christian Lord. But this is unnecessary, as long as the reader acknowledges the distinction.

THE 'SYNOPTIC' GOSPELS

Why are there four gospels? The simple answer is that four writings about the life, death and resurrection of Jesus Christ came into being, each acquiring apostolic authority. No canon of writings would have been acceptable to the whole Church that omitted any of these. But many other 'gospels' were written, of which the texts have survived, hidden for centuries. Despite differences in their accounts, the canonical gospels together were accepted and deviating accounts deemed heretical.

In fact, the consensus between the four gospels is not particularly impressive. There are really just two gospel portraits, of which one exists in three editions. Matthew, Mark and Luke exhibit the same structure, share a great deal of content and, broadly, depict the same life. Consequently, they are known as the 'Synoptic Gospels'; that is, they share a common viewpoint. Without entering into scholarly debates, we can follow the majority view that Matthew and Luke are almost certainly expansions of the earliest and shortest gospel, Mark. The precise dates of these gospels are unknown, but Mark is generally set either just before or just after 70, when Jerusalem fell to the Romans, with Matthew and Luke a few decades afterwards. Some of their expansions of Mark—especially sayings—are also shared, pointing to a common source, while each also has its own special material. It seems sensible, then, to abandon canonical order and begin with Mark's Gospel.

The Gospel of Mark

We owe the word 'gospel' to Mark, which opens with 'The beginning of the gospel (*euaggelion*) of Jesus Christ, the Son of God'. Just as with Revelation, the opening word (*apocalypsis*) apparently became a title for the literary genre. 'Gospel' means 'good news', but is the 'good news' *what* Jesus preached, or is *he* the good news? That is a very interesting question, for in the New Testament, as in the history of Christianity, emphasis has tended to be placed on one rather than the other, either the exemplary message of the 'kingdom of God' or the death of Jesus. Did Jesus come into the world primarily to teach or to die, to educate or to redeem? Mark and his fellow Synoptic evangelists deal with both facets, but Matthew and Luke give more space to teaching than does Mark. Paul's letters, earlier than all the gospels, demonstrate no interest at all in his Lord's teachings.

The Mark to whom this gospel is attributed is probably the person mentioned in Acts 12 and 15 as a friend of Barnabas, both of whom joined Paul for a while. But apparently Mark left them and Paul would not take him on another journey. He is mentioned again in Colossians (where he is named as Barnabas's nephew), 2 Timothy and Philemon, and thus may have been reconciled with Paul. In 1 Peter, greetings are sent from 'my son Mark', possibly the same person, though Mark (Marcus, Markos) was a common name. The reference in 1 Peter, at any rate, gave rise to a story from Papias, bishop of Hierapolis in Asia Minor (ca. 60–130 CE), that this gospel was really dictated by Peter. This is most likely an attempt to give it apostolic authority. Yet Peter's memory would surely have been better than this gospel suggests. Would he not have remembered, for example, seeing the risen Jesus? Or did he not witness it?

For, as an account of Jesus's life, Mark's Gospel is highly compressed. We shall set it out here because it displays the basic plan followed by the two other Synoptic Gospels, for which we need only note the main differences.

Mark fits Jesus's ministry, starting with his baptism by John, within a single year, devoting over a third of his text (chapters 11–16) to the final week of Jesus's life on earth. The baptism of Jesus is introduced by a link to the Jewish scriptures:

> As it is written in the prophet Isaiah,
> 'See, I am sending my messenger ahead of you,
> who will prepare your way;
> the voice of one crying out in the wilderness:
> "Prepare the way of the Lord, make his paths straight"'

In fact, only the second part of the quotation comes from Isaiah, the first being from Malachi. But the 'voice in the wilderness' is John the Baptizer, who announces one greater to come. Jesus is baptized, the spirit descends on him and a heavenly voice proclaims him 'my son', as Jesus is also identified in the opening verse. 'Son of God' recurs four more times in the gospel, including as a kind of epitaph from a centurion at the cross (15:39). But Mark also uses 'son of man' and 'son of David', prompting the reader to wonder as whose son we should see him? Is Mark unsure, or trying to fuse the different titles into a single profile? He also uses 'Christ' (twice), while 'Messiah' (of which 'Christ' is a literal translation) is used by others but never affirmed by Jesus. How Mark assesses the true nature of Jesus is one of several puzzles in his gospel.

After baptism, Jesus goes into the wilderness and is tempted by the devil, then calls disciples and begins teaching and healing in Galilee. He forgives the sins of a paralyzed man before curing him, incurring opposition from scribes and Pharisees. Dining with a tax-collector and his friends causes Pharisees more offence. Here, we can already see where blame will lie for Jesus's death. Crucifixion was a Roman punishment, but in a gospel written for Roman subjects it was an unpromising admission: better that the Roman authorities were reluctant, and allowed the execution under pressure from the Jewish leaders who later rebelled against Rome. The blame is spread between several religious groups: Pharisees, scribes, Herodians and priests (the Sadducees, curiously, are implicated only in Matthew's Gospel). But the antagonism starts early on.

Jesus's ministry follows a pattern of collecting followers, gathering crowds, healing, exorcising demons and giving offence to established religious groups. The pace is fast, with little detail, almost like a set of notes. Jesus also teaches, mainly in parables. Here arises a second puzzle: the parables seem on the one hand a simple way of illustrating a point. But the disciples do not understand! In chapter 4, for example, comes the parable of the sower. But afterwards (verses 10-13):

> When he was alone, those who were around him along with the twelve asked him about the parables.
>
> And he said to them, 'To you has been given the secret of the kingdom of God, but for those outside, everything comes in parables; in order that "they may indeed look, but not perceive, and may indeed listen, but not understand"; so as to change their ways and be forgiven.'" And he said to them, 'Do you not understand this parable? Then how will you understand all the parables?'

And then the parable is explained. But were Jesus's teachings *really* not understood by most people? Or did Jesus's followers cultivate the notion of secret meanings for the initiated only?

Jesus's miracles in Mark include the reviving of the dead daughter of Jairus (perhaps alluding to Elijah's reviving of a widow's son in 1 Kings 17), after which he sends his disciples out to heal, exorcise and to call people to repentance. Repentance had also been the message of John the Baptizer, reinforced by the warning that the 'kingdom of God' was coming. But much of Jesus's teaching about the kingdom represents it as something to be entered or accepted, as if it were something available now, and not some kind of future visitation to be feared. This further ambiguity in the gospel extends to the whole of the New Testament—and indeed through two thousand years of Christianity. On the one hand is an expectation that divine retribution will soon come, with the return of Jesus to earth; on the other hand is an affirmation that the kingdom is already here, within the community of Christian believers. Most theologians will (understandably) say that both are correct!

In Mark, Jesus's death is intimated in several ways before the final events of his life are actually narrated. The gruesome story of the death of John the Baptizer in Mark 6 is a first hint, followed soon after by further disputes with Pharisees and scribes. But what do the teachings and these miracles *signify*? This question seems to have been anticipated, for in 8:27 Jesus asks his disciples who people think he is. After receiving different answers, he asks Peter (Simon), who replies 'the Messiah', a reply that he is warned to keep to himself. But Peter, James and John then go with Jesus to a mountain, where they see him become dazzling white (typically the appearance of angelic beings) and flanked by Moses and Elijah. Why these two? Perhaps because of the curious circumstance of the end of their lives: Moses's grave is a secret, while Elijah ascends to heaven. If so, Jesus's

ascension might be indicated (though it is not described in the gospel). Or
do they represent the Law and Prophets that Jesus fulfils? Jesus is, at any
rate, again called 'my beloved son' from above, and again orders the disciples to say nothing 'until the son of man had risen from the dead'. We now
have a stronger hint of what is to come and also learn Jesus's preferred self-
designation. But unfortunately, it settles very little of our curiosity. The
term basically means 'human', and is how God addresses the prophet
Ezekiel; in Daniel, though, it refers to a divinity; and it was also used as
a deprecating or polite form of self-reference. All these possibilities have
been endlessly debated. On arriving in Jerusalem, Jesus will be hailed as
'son of David' (10:47-48; see 12:35), and although the title is not explicitly
endorsed by either Jesus or Mark, the entry into Jerusalem on a colt apparently fulfils a prophecy in Zechariah 9:9:

> Look, your king comes to you;
> triumphant and victorious is he,
> humble and riding on a donkey,
> on a colt, the foal of a donkey.

The next day, Jesus lays a curse on a fig tree that was fruitless because
it was out of season. This unreasonable action begs for a symbolic interpretation: that the Jews (or some Jews) are fruitless? That would fit with
the parable of the vineyard tenants who kill the owner's son, which comes
immediately after the forcible removal of moneychangers in the Temple.
This could hardly have been a single-handed feat (as it is so often painted),
and it is not obvious, either, that his targets were doing anything wrong.
Temple dues were paid only in Tyrian shekels, so changing currency was
often necessary; and the business was lawful. Many readers deduce that
the exchange rate was distorted, but Mark does not say so. For the first
time, at any rate, Jesus is taking violent action, the point of which is not
really clear, but what we might call 'mob violence' is probably involved.
No wonder the scribes and chief priests now question his authority for
acting thus and want to kill him. His death looms as a woman anoints his
head ('messiah' means 'anointed'), which Jesus interprets as if washing his
corpse. Mark's Gospel is often viewed as unsubtle, but with its numerous
foreshadowings, the build-up to the climax is worthy of Alfred Hitchcock.

Writing (probably) just after the fall of the temple to the Roman general Titus—publicly commemorated in Rome—the point is being made
that divine judgment on the 'den of robbers' has been executed. This is
made clear by the following 'prophecy', called by scholars the 'Markan

apocalypse', in which Jesus foretells the destruction of Jerusalem and of ensuing persecutions and trials, 'false messiahs and prophets', then a cosmic event, when the 'son of man' will descend with clouds—alluding to Daniel's scenario of the final kingdom. But is this a political kingdom? What are Jesus's own ambitions? After the events of Judas's betrayal, the Passover meal, and Jesus's arrest comes a trial before the 'chief priests' and the 'council' (the Sanhedrin, the supreme Jewish court). Here, Jesus answers to being both Messiah and 'Son of Man'. But before the Roman prefect, Pilate, he does not answer to the title 'king of the Jews', and Pilate, reluctant to condemn Jesus, offers a release. Barabbas being chosen for release instead, Jesus is crucified under the sign 'king of the Jews'. Such a verdict is embarrassing enough for the gospel to make it historically probable. Mark presents Pilate as reluctantly conceding to this condemnation—which does not fit what we know of Pilate! But no theological explanation for Jesus's death emerges very clearly from this gospel. The titles 'Son of God', 'Messiah', 'son of David' and 'Son of Man' give no clue. Paul had given his answer, but made no use of these titles.

The most striking of Mark's mysteries comes at the very end. Jesus's body is placed in the tomb of Joseph, and two days afterwards, three women—his mother, Mary of Magdala and Salome—come to anoint the body but encounter a young man in a white robe (the traditional garb of an angel) who states that Jesus is not here but has gone ahead to Galilee. They leave in terror, telling no one. Here, according to the two oldest bibles, Sinaiticus and Vaticanus, the gospel ends. But Alexandrinus and Ephraemi Rescriptus from a century later contain the ending that modern bibles now provide in 16:9-20. This ending may have been extracted from Matthew and Luke. An alternative, shorter ending is also found in some early manuscripts. The mystery of the ending, however, remains. If there really was more written, how did it become lost?

The Gospel of Matthew

Matthew is traditionally identified with the disciple Levi, the tax-collector. But about two thirds of the gospel of Matthew is taken from Mark, with identical or near-identical wording and the same outline of Jesus's life. Additionally, almost a quarter of the gospel consists of sayings of Jesus that are paralleled in Luke, leading to a widely held scholarly theory that both gospels utilized an earlier collection. The name given to this collection is Q (German *Quelle* = 'source'). Why could an eyewitness not supply his own story? But what Matthew has added or reorganized is quite distinctive.

The sayings of Jesus are gathered into five discourses (chapters 5–7, 10, 13, 18 and 23–25), a device perhaps intended to present Jesus as a new Moses, especially when the first one is set on a mountain. Consistent with this presentation is a story modelled on Moses's own birth (Exodus 1), with Herod rather than Pharaoh ordering the killing of newborn males. This 'second Moses', however, comes not to end the law, but to fulfil it (5:17). He also fulfils much Old Testament prophecy, which the gospel regularly cites.

Matthew makes harsh condemnation of 'scribes and Pharisees', those Jews especially concerned with the meaning and observance of the Law. But he goes further in the way he exonerates Pilate of blame from Jesus's death and in 27:25 transfers it to the Jewish crowd: 'his blood be upon us and our children', they cry. We need not doubt that Matthew's readers had washed their own hands of Judaism.

Other features unique to Matthew are the stories of birth and death. The birth story removes the ambiguity of Mark's 'Son of God' title, and has Mary and Joseph apparently living in Bethlehem from the outset but fleeing to Egypt (reversing the Exodus but enabling another Old Testament prophecy to be cited) and returning to Nazareth to avoid Herod. To this story belong the star and the wise men from the East. In the account of Jesus's death come unique details such as the opening of the graves of the righteous and the posting of guards at the tomb. The gospel ends with Jesus's commission to his disciples to make converts from all the nations, again turning away from the Jews.

The Gospel of Luke

The Gospel of Luke is traditionally (and by most scholars) attributed to Luke because the author of Acts claims that Acts was written as a sequel to an account of the life of Jesus, that is, this gospel. In Acts, the author identifies himself as accompanying Paul on occasions and Luke is referred to in Colossians 4:14 (as the 'beloved physician'), in 2 Timothy 4:11 and in Philemon 24, though only the last of these letters is generally considered genuinely from Paul (see Chapter 9). There is, however, an intriguing question about the date of the two volumes. Acts ends with Paul still alive in Rome, which might suggest it was written some time before 70, by which time he is thought to have been executed. But this would make the gospel—the earlier volume—earlier than Mark's, which, as explained earlier, is unlikely. The obvious conclusion is that Acts was written well after Paul's death but intended to finish on an optimistic note.

Like Matthew, this gospel relates Jesus to the Old Testament, but less by citing individual 'prophecies' and more by presenting the whole of scripture as narrating a divine plan. So, the ending of Acts is likely inspired by the ending of Kings, where the deported king is released from confinement to be a royal guest. Like Matthew, the writer used Mark and the collection of sayings known as Q, adding his own distinctive material, especially parables (look between chapters 10 and 18). There are also differences in the narrative of Jesus's birth and death. According to Luke, Mary and Joseph live in Nazareth and travel to Bethlehem for a census. No wise men are present, only shepherds. The birth of John the Baptizer, presented here as a priestly relative of Jesus, is also announced. A story of Jesus's childhood visit to Jerusalem is added.

Both Matthew and Luke have a genealogy of Jesus through David, but Matthew goes forward from Abraham, while Luke works backwards to Adam, as if to emphasize Jesus's universality rather than his Jewishness. The genealogies list different names but both run through Joseph, not Mary. So, if Joseph was not Jesus's biological father, they have no *literal* value. Or possibly a belief in divine parentage had not yet become fully articulated, and what was envisaged is rather the kind of miraculous conception of Isaac by Sarah or Samuel by Hannah. The song of Mary after the visit of Gabriel is, after all, modelled on Hannah's in 1 Samuel 1. But the genealogies are symbolic, anyway, and fit the interests of the gospel writer. Matthew has Jesus challenging the claim to Abrahamic ancestry of Sadducees and Pharisees (3:9) that 'God is able from these stones to raise up children to Abraham'. Luke may want rather to highlight Jesus's universality as a 'second Adam'. The precise nature of Jesus's genetic makeup generated furious controversy in later Christianity, but the gospel writers seem not to want to go there.

Luke's unique contributions to the Jesus story include several parables (the 'Good Samaritan', the 'Prodigal Son'), an extra trial before 'Herod' and a resurrection appearance to two men on the Emmaus road. The gospel also concludes, uniquely, with the ascension of Jesus, after which the disciples 'worshipped him' and 'continued blessing God in the Temple', setting the scene for the opening of Acts. Several interactions with women (e.g. 7:36-50; 8:2-3; 10:38-42; 23:27-28) might suggest that the churches for which the gospel was written had a high female membership. An ancient, but improbable tradition developed that Luke derived some of his material from Jesus's mother.

The Gospel of John

The author of the Gospel of John claims to be Jesus's 'beloved disciple', and John has long been identified with him. But even if there were such a disciple (the Synoptics make no mention of such a person), he is not a likely candidate. Just possibly it is the John of the book of Revelation, or a 'John the Elder' who was mentioned by some of the early Fathers of the church. The author of the New Testament letters of John is another candidate. But scholars suspect, from the unevenness of the composition, that there was more than one author.

The gospel is quite unlike the Synoptics, both in historical detail and in its portrayal of Jesus. It relates a three-year ministry, which seems more plausible than a single year, and includes more than one visit to Jerusalem. Another important chronological difference is the placing of the crucifixion on the fifth day of the week (Thursday), prior to the Passover festival itself. So, the Last Supper is not a Passover meal and there is no Eucharistic ceremony. Instead, Jesus washes the disciples' feet. More differences from the Synoptics emerge in the crucifixion (what Jesus says, and, notably the blood and water mixed: these are the agents of purification in Jewish ritual). Also, Mary of Magdala sees him first outside the tomb, and the disciple Thomas later has his doubts removed ('blessed are those who have not seen and yet believe' is the message to the reader).

The gospel is full of symbolic allusions to Judaism: a non-literal reading is necessary to seize the sense. There are seven miracles, which here are called 'signs', including turning water into wine at Cana and raising Lazarus from the dead. But in seven discourses, Jesus declares directly (quite contrary to the Synoptics) what he understands himself and his mission to be ('I am...')—though he does so by using metaphors. He comes into conflict not with 'scribes and Pharisees', but with 'the Jews'. At the end of chapter 8, the Jews are denounced as 'offspring of Satan'. So the gospel reflects a more complete separation from Judaism than Matthew, suggesting a relatively late dating (not before the end of the first century CE). Some scholars have recently tried to argue that 'Judeans' may be meant. The Greek word is the same. But this is not a natural interpretation in this context, and the gospel is hardly a rejection of Judea! We must accept that this rejection was part of the formation of many emerging Christian identities! This does not oblige the reader to endorse it.

The difference between John and the Synoptics is actually fundamental. While the Synoptics stress Jesus's humanity, John's gospel stresses his divinity. There is no birth narrative: instead, the writer introduces Jesus as the eternal Word (Greek *logos*) of God, made human to show the divine glory. This *logos* is a philosophical concept of Stoics and Platonists, being a universal principle that mediates between the 'One' or the 'Good' (or 'God') and the human soul. The first century CE Jewish philosopher Philo used it in interpreting the Law allegorically. There are similar Old Testament concepts, too. The book of Proverbs describes a personified (female!) Wisdom, present with God at creation. God's creative speech in Genesis 1, and his communication with the prophets, was concretized by the Jewish rabbis as his 'Word' (*memra* in Aramaic). This is a fine example of how Jewish and Greek thought could be, and were, integrated. The author of John's Gospel, in making his Jesus a cosmic figure, draws on both cultures.

This gospel also makes a direct offer to its readers. 'But these are written so that you may come to believe that Jesus is the Messiah, the Son of God, and that through believing you may have life in his name' (20:31). Those who believe will not 'taste death'. In the Synoptics, this phrase means that the kingdom will come within one's lifetime. But in John, 'eternal life' is qualitatively different, more in line with what the apostle Paul offers his hearers: an escape, already secured, from the power of death. The kingdom is a dimension of being, which John's Jesus brings to his followers.

Why is this gospel so different from the Synoptics? Did the author know these other gospels? There are enough similarities to suggest that he did. But he ends: 'This is the disciple who is testifying to these things and has written them, and we know that his testimony is true'. Yet is this really an eyewitness gospel any more than the others? Are these things 'true'—and the Synoptics therefore 'false'? The modern reader needs to understand that we are confronted with different responses to the figure of Jesus. The 'Jesus of history' who might have resolved such a question is beyond our own reach—as he was already beyond the gospel writers and their readers.

Chapter Eight
The Acts of the Apostles

'In the first book, Theophilus, I wrote about all that Jesus began to do and teach'. So Acts begins, picking up where the Gospel of Luke ends, with Jesus's appearances to the apostles and his ascension. Jesus's work will continue through the Holy Spirit. Jesus's life brought him from Galilee to Jerusalem; the Spirit will lead from Jerusalem to Rome, from the Jewish capital to the imperial capital, universalizing the gospel. Acts is the only scriptural narrative we have of Christian origins, though the letters of Paul supply some autobiographical information. Its main aim is not factual history, but 'sacred history', like the Old Testament, and its historical reliability, which is hard to assess, is not particularly important. Luke was a companion of Paul but did not necessarily witness all that he relates. The maps of Paul's 'missionary journeys' probably reflect the author's arrangement of different pieces of information—places visited, journeys made—into a scheme, which is not always straightforward to follow (18:24-19:7 is a good example).

The first part of Luke's story focuses on the figures of Peter and Paul. Peter represents the link to Jerusalem, to Jesus's own life and to the Jewish world, while Paul represents a link to the heavenly Christ and the destination of the gospel in the Roman Empire. The largely negative portrayal of Jewish reception of the gospel is probably correct, but the point is theological rather than historical. The largely positive portrait of Roman reaction (already evident in the gospels) is diplomatic. The breakout from a Jewish to a universal gospel is described in largely consensual terms and as Spirit-driven. The impression we gather from Paul's letters is rather less collegial. But we must not necessarily accept Paul's word: he has his own interests, too.

JERUSALEM

The first part of Acts establishes continuity between Jesus and the apostles. The apostolic core of twelve apostles is maintained by electing a replacement for Judas (whose death is reported differently from Matthew 27:5 where it is characteristically fitted to a scriptural prophecy). The story continues with the coming of the Holy Spirit on the disciples at Pentecost, bestowing the gift of prophecy. Luke seems to understand this as 'speaking in tongues', a strange speech. Paul clearly distinguishes the two. But Luke is establishing an Old Testament precedent. A speech that everyone can understand reverses the Tower of Babel story in Genesis 11, where God divided the unified human race into different languages so that they could not understand each other. Peter's speech to the crowds, like all the speeches in Acts, is composed by Luke and cites passages from Joel 2:28-32 predicting the outpouring of the Spirit (Acts 2:17-21), Psalm 16:8-11 (Acts 2:25-28) and Psalm 110:1 (Acts 2:34-35). Acts shows, as did the gospel, how well Luke knows his scriptures and how effectively he uses them to join the story of Jesus Christ to the story of Israel and produce a story of humanity.

A story in 4:32-5:11 about communal possession of property and support for the poor may seem digressive, but, again, it has an Old Testament antecedent. Ananias withholds some proceeds of a sale that should have gone to the community fund. In doing so, he recapitulates the behaviour of Achan in Joshua 7, and with the same outcome, his own death and the death of his wife (who, this time, is guilty as well). Ananias is another Achan, but also the Christian community is a new Israel, too. Unlike some other New Testament authors, Luke is not an unqualified Jew-basher. He pointedly comments, for instance, that the Pharisee Gamaliel (a celebrated figure in rabbinic tradition, too) rescues the apostles from execution by convincing the court that 'If this is from God, you will be unable to stop them' (5:39). Later, in 18:8, we are told also of Crispus, a synagogue leader, who 'believed in the Lord'. Such Jews exist and are welcomed (though see below on Stephen's speech). But Luke is critical of the way Jews cannot accept what he regards as the meaning of their own scriptures.

BEYOND JERUSALEM

The mission now spreads outside Palestine and interest shifts (chapter 6) from Aramaic-speaking Jewish followers towards Greek speakers, as a step towards reaching out to non-Jews. Seven assistants ('deacons') are appointed, following complaints from the 'Greeks' about the distribution of welfare, and 'deacons' are appointed to take care of such practicalities. One of these is called Stephen, who does not confine himself to his practical tasks but preaches and heals with great success, and is accused of blasphemy. Stephen's long speech (again written by Luke) is an anti-Jewish diatribe, extensively invoking the scriptures, selecting Abraham, Moses and David and accusing 'you stubborn people, uncircumcised in heart and ears' of 'resisting the Holy Spirit' and murdering the 'righteous one'. His subsequent stoning is hardly unexpected, and his clothes are laid at the feet of one called Saul, who then begins to hunt down 'the church'.

The members of the 'church' scatter from Judea. The apostle Philip makes converts in Samaria, then, on the way to Gaza, converts and baptizes an Ethiopian Jew. Some believers have fled beyond Palestine to Damascus, where Saul (chapter 9) travels to seek them out. On the way, he famously undergoes an experience that leaves him blind and convinces him that the one whose followers he is harassing has spoken to him from heaven. Now he proclaims Jesus as 'Son of God' and 'the Christ'. He preaches in Damascus and Jerusalem, but for his own safety is finally sent to Caesarea.

Questions about non-Jewish converts shifts attention back to Peter. The tension between 'Hebrew' (Aramaic-speakers) and 'Greek' Jews gives way to relations between Jewish and non-Jewish Christians. How far can these live together in Christian communities? Paul's letters suggest a serious, ongoing disagreement over this, but Luke tells us how Peter comes to his own conclusion. He goes to Joppa (Jaffa), near Caesarea, where lives 'a devout man who feared God with all his household' (10:2) and who is later described as 'well spoken of by the Jewish people' (10:22). This man, a Roman soldier called Cornelius, occupies a significant space: on the boundary between Jew and non-Jew. Cornelius dreams of an angel who commands him to summon Peter. On the way to Joppa, Peter has a dream of various animals on a tablecloth, including those unclean in Jewish law. Three times he is told to kill and eat, and three times he refuses (the reader will think of Peter's threefold denial of Jesus in Luke 22). Cornelius's men find Peter, who goes with them on his first visit to a non-Jewish house. He now understands the dream and converts the household, and the principle is established that Jews and non-Jews will eat together at the Christian table. In Jerusalem, he defends his actions and persuades the other apostles of the mission to non-Jews. That Peter reaches the same view on non-Jewish conversion as Paul, and does so independently, is important for Luke, even if Paul wants to take more credit for himself and in Galatians accuses Peter of backsliding on the issue.

ANTIOCH

The mission to non-Jews will be based in a Syrian city with a significant Jewish population. We are introduced to Barnabas, a Levite from Cyprus who was originally called Joseph (Acts 4:36). He summons Paul from Tarsus (Paul's hometown) and they remain in Antioch for a year. In this city, adds Luke, the word 'Christian' is first used.

The action shifts for one last time away from Paul. In Jerusalem, Herod Agrippa's execution of the apostle James is followed by Peter's imprisonment. But Peter is escorted from prison by an angel, to the house of John Mark. Herod, by contrast, is heckled by crowds and then 'eaten by worms'. This sounds very much more like the death of his grandfather, Herod the Great, but there is confusion in the New Testament between the members of the Herodian family (see Chart 2 in Chapter 6).

From now on, the story is all about Paul and is structured as a journey towards Rome in three major 'missionary journeys' that lead up to a final voyage from Caesarea to the imperial capital. The movement towards Rome will involve many cities of Asia Minor (modern Turkey) and Greece, and the names of fellow-workers will be mentioned. Jews will largely resist the message, and Paul and his companions will run into trouble many times, often rescued by Roman officials. There are opportunities, too, for Luke to supply sermons on scriptural fulfilment (e.g. 13:16-47).

The 'first missionary journey' of Paul and Barnabas is followed up with a second visit (see Map 6). But before any more journeys are undertaken, the question of non-Jews has to be formally resolved. Jewish Christians maintained that converts must be circumcised, that is, become fully Jewish and subject to the Mosaic law. Peter, Paul and Barnabas resist this. At a meeting scholars refer to as the 'council of Jerusalem', the issue is settled by the leader of the movement, James, identified by Paul in Galatians 1:19 as the 'brother of the Lord'. (It's interesting that this highly important figure is entirely unmentioned in the gospels.) James's compromise is that non-Jewish Christians should abstain from food declared unclean by Jews, from meat containing blood and from sexual immorality. Actually, these were conditions that Jews laid on 'righteous' non-Jews as their 'law' and are referred to in Jewish sources as the 'covenant of Noah' (see Genesis 9). A letter to this effect is taken to Antioch and its daughter churches. Paul's letters suggest that the issue remained disputed, which we can well imagine. Not long afterwards, Paul and his new companion Silas are joined by Timothy, the son of a Jewish mother and non-Jewish father. Paul has him circumcised 'because of the Jews', 'for they all knew his father was Greek' (16:3).

Map 6: Paul's first journey (Acts 13–14)

The second journey (see Map 7) takes Paul and his associates to Europe—Macedonia then Greece. At this point, Luke briefly uses 'we'. At Philippi, 'they' are thrown into prison but convert the jailer, who is baptized along with his family. From this we learn that baptism is the conversion rite (see Chapter 9). From Thessalonica and Berea, Paul proceeds alone to Athens, making a famous speech, more philosophical than scriptural, proclaiming the nature of the 'unknown god' (17:22-31). The reception is cool, especially towards the idea of resurrection, which to philosophically-minded Greeks was a gross idea.

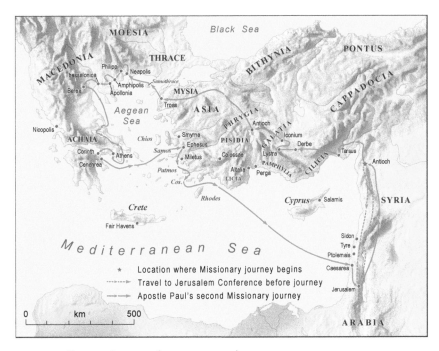

Map 7: Paul's second journey (Acts 15:36-18:22)

In Corinth, the next stop, Paul stays with a married couple, Priscilla and Aquila, finally running into trouble again and being taken before Gallio. But, like a good Roman official, he rejects the charges and Paul returns to Antioch.

The 'third missionary journey' takes Paul back to Galatia and Phrygia and (apparently) to Corinth again, where (chapter 18) we meet Apollos from Alexandria. The interesting thing about him is that he knew of Jesus but only 'the baptism of John'—a rare clue that John the Baptizer had a following outside Judea. After proper instruction he becomes a formidable preacher, but Paul meets more people like this in Ephesus. The issue here is again about Judaism as a stage towards Christianity.

Map 8: Paul's third journey (Acts 18:23-20:38)

This journey is completed with visits to Corinth and Ephesus, then back to Antioch via Caesarea and Jerusalem.

The 'third missionary journey' included a prolonged stay in Ephesus. Here, the makers of religious objects for the local goddess Artemis (the Roman Diana) accuse Paul of ruining their business by denouncing her cult. Again, a city official dismisses the crowd. But a rumoured Jewish plot persuades Paul to return by land to Philippi in Thrace and then by ship to Troas. At this point, more and more of his companions are named, perhaps because Luke is now part of the action. He resumes speaking of 'we' during the journey, down the coast of Asia as far as Miletus, where Paul summoned the leaders of the Ephesus church, whom he addresses as if he will never see them again. Then the group sail to Caesarea, heading for Jerusalem.

In Caesarea, Paul is warned that he will be handed over to the 'Gentiles' once in Jerusalem, and Paul replies by stating his willingness to die, saying 'The Lord's will be done' (compare Luke 22:42 of Jesus). The events of Jesus's last days, though in many ways different, are hinted at in Paul's last visit to Jerusalem. But first comes a meeting between James, in charge of converting Jews, and Paul, who has created non-Jewish churches. One problem had not been dealt with—and it touched Paul personally: what about Jews who became Christians? Were they still to be subject to the law? Paul agonizes over this in some of his letters but answers now by agreeing to perform a Jewish cultic ceremony. But then 'Jews from Asia' stir up a crowd and Paul is apprehended. He addresses the crowd in Aramaic (chapter 22) and tells the story of his call from Jesus. At the crowd's angry response, he is taken into Roman custody, where he announces his Roman citizenship. Before the Sanhedrin, he claims to be on trial for his belief in resurrection, an issue on which Pharisaic and Sadducean members of the court would disagree. So, no outcome, and he is taken back into Roman custody, and, on discovery of a Jewish plot to kill him, is sent to the Roman procurator, Felix, in Caesarea.

Paul, unlike Jesus, has been rescued from Jews by the Roman authorities but is to be in Roman hands for the rest of the story. The procurator Felix procrastinates—the impression is given that he is interested in Paul's message—but is succeeded by Festus, who conducts more hearings before sending Paul to Rome. But first he makes an appearance before a Herod— the son of the Herod Agrippa who had disposed of James, an event reminiscent of Jesus's own trial before another Herod (unique to Luke, probably invented). But Paul takes yet another opportunity to offer his testimonial. Agrippa, half-Jew, half Roman, finds nothing reprehensible: Paul, he says, could have been released if he had not appealed to Caesar. But Jewish hostility and Roman uncertainty (not to mention the Holy Spirit) have placed Paul in custody and heading for Rome.

PAUL'S JOURNEY TO ROME

How reliable Luke's account of Paul's eventful journey is we cannot know, but he writes again as if he were there. The climax is a shipwreck, evoking stories about Jonah and Jesus. On Malta, his immunity to a snakebite and his cures are virtues typically attached to magicians and wonder-workers of the ancient world. But eventually he arrives in Rome and, under house arrest, wastes little time in summoning the local Jewish leaders. Knowing nothing of him other than rumours, they come, and he explains that he is 'in chains' for the 'hope of Israel'. Attempts to convince them end with only partial success and Paul denounces them, asserting the great theme of Acts, that 'God's salvation' has been sent to non-Jews. This brings the book almost to a close: the final two verses state simply the happy ending that Paul stayed in his own rented accommodation, preaching 'with no hindrance'.

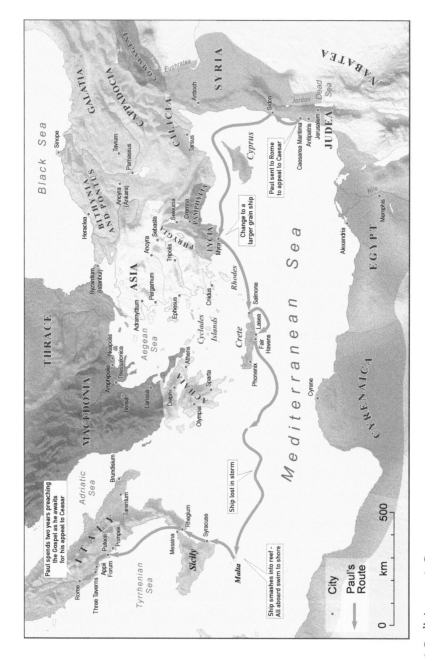

Map 9: Paul's journey to Rome

THE SPEECHES OF ACTS: FROM THE SCRIPTURES TO PAUL

As said earlier, Luke follows the custom of historians and uses speeches not as verbatim records of what was said, but as a means of explaining how the reader is to understand either the character's motivations or the significance of his story. In the early part of Acts, all the speeches, including Paul's, focus on the scriptural witness to Jesus. But as Paul's career advances, his speeches focus on his own history and destiny. He underlines how Jesus himself commanded him to evangelize. This line from Jesus *directly* to Paul is a challenge to the other apostles who had known the earthly Jesus. Paul's final speech to the Jews of Rome, in which he preaches from the 'law of Moses and the prophets', ends with a citation from Isaiah 6:9-10 that prophesies their stubbornness of heart, eyes and ears; the Jews' own scriptures have condemned them. This prophecy is, however, applied to Paul's own situation. His mission, like that of Jesus, is foretold in scripture. The coolness of the Jewish reception is quite understandable, but the boldest option is to explain it as already foretold. The gospel of Jesus and its rejection by Judaism are *both* fulfilling the scriptures. How could the Jews win?

ca. 33–36	Vision of heavenly Jesus on the road from Jerusalem to Damascus; spends three years in Arabia; returns to Damascus to preach.
ca. 36	Flees from Damascus; meets the apostles in Jerusalem.
36–44	Preaches in Tarsus and surrounding region.
44–46	Teaches in Antioch with Barnabas.
46	With Barnabas visits Jerusalem with famine relief offering.
47–48	First missionary journey with Barnabas.
49	At 'Council of Jerusalem', secures agreement that Gentile Christians need not follow Jewish law; returns to Antioch and confronts Peter over the same issue.
49–52	Second missionary journey with Silas, through Asia Minor and Greece; settles in Corinth.
52	Visits Jerusalem and Antioch; third missionary journey.
52–55	Stays in Ephesus.
55–57	Travels through Greece.
57–59	Returns to Jerusalem, arrested, imprisoned at Caesarea.
59–60	Appears before Felix, Festus and Herod, appeals to Caesar; sent to Rome.
60–	Under house arrest at Rome.

Chronology of Paul's Life

Chapter Nine

The New Testament Letters

The New Testament letters illuminate how the story of Jesus Christ became embedded in the life of Christian communities, while expectation of the return of the Christ diminished and attention was directed to living in the here and now in ways that the gospel demanded. The ethical norms encouraged here are not conspicuously out of line with Jewish ones, or even most non-Jewish ones. Solidarity is, of course, important—a requirement of threatened minorities. The attention paid in the Synoptic Gospels to Jesus's own lifestyle perhaps betrays an increasing interest in Christian virtue: care for the poor and sick, spreading the good news, fighting evil forces in the world, resisting the temptation of Satan, suffering what must be suffered.

The order of New Testament letters, originally variable, is now fixed, with Paul first, then James, Peter, John and Jude. Paul's letters to churches come first, in order of length, followed by personal letters and, finally, a letter 'to the Hebrews' which does not bear Paul's name and was not initially attributed to him. Because the thoughts expressed in these writings are sometimes hard to untangle, a chronological approach will allow us more easily to detect changes of mind or of emphasis. Inevitably, centuries of Christian interpretation have assembled a coherent Pauline 'theology', but in reflecting on his eventful career and the radical issues that he confronted, we would hardly expect a coherent position to emerge fully worked out from the beginning. Paul did not merely preach the gospel; he continually strove to define it.

Three important general considerations need bearing in mind. First, these letters are written to and for individual communities with different characteristics and concerns. Of necessity, the letters are ad hoc. Although subsequently used as such, they were not originally meant to offer permanent answers to universal questions. And certainly not for readers two thousand years later! But they would have been read out in many Christian gatherings—perhaps in instalments, perhaps more than once—and obviously were preserved and disseminated.

Second, these letters, as authoritative Christian scripture, will almost certainly have been amended for a variegated Christian membership. This process we can sometimes detect but we cannot measure how far the preserved texts conform to the originals. Third, some of the letters attributed to Paul do not fit what he says or how he writes in his other letters, and must be judged pseudepigraphic. Paul's writings were sufficiently well known to invite imitation, though there is no consensus on every one of these dubious letters. In the case of those to Timothy, we may actually have parts of genuine writings interspersed with later additions. From such letters it becomes clear that the authority of Paul was invoked to promote ideas that he may not have endorsed.

Yet, while the authorship of the letters is historically important, and belief in Paul's authorship may have influenced the canonicity of a particular letter, the theological implications are negligible. What matters is that those who determined the New Testament canon regarded their contents as true to the apostolic gospel.

The main topics in Paul's letters on which we can concentrate are those highlighted in Acts: Paul's understanding of the significance of Jesus and the place of Jews and Judaism alongside non-Jews in the Christian communities and in the divine plan for humanity. We shall note that his letters do not always confirm what Acts relates about him. In most cases, preference should probably be given to the letters, but with due caution; Paul is no less concerned about his image than any other influential leader!

The other letters are of importance in qualifying Paul's domination of the New Testament story of Jesus. Paul may exert an overwhelming influence but this does not mean that within early Christian communities— only a few of which he himself founded—a single coherent set of beliefs and practices emerged.

THE LETTERS OF PAUL

Authentic letters

These letters do not necessarily contain exactly the words written (or dictated) by Paul, and some may be a mixture of more than one letter. But they are sufficiently consistent and coherent in style and content to make them 'Pauline'. The order of their writing is not entirely certain, since we cannot always establish from where they were sent.

To the church in Thessalonica

Although Acts relates only a brief visit of a few weeks to Thessalonica, a major seaport of northern Greece (17:1-10), the two letters to the Thessalonians imply a longer acquaintance, given what the Christian community there managed to achieve, and Paul's own recollection of practising his trade as a tentmaker in the city.

Possibly the second letter is not really from Paul. Its contents are characteristic enough, but its tone is very different from the first letter. Here, we give it the benefit of the doubt. The earlier letter (probably written around 50 CE) expresses Paul's bitter rejection of 'the Jews' (1 Thessalonians 2:14-16).

> For you, brothers and sisters, became imitators of the churches of God in Christ Jesus in Judea, for you suffered the same things from your own compatriots as they did from the Jews, who killed both the Lord Jesus and the prophets, and drove us out; they displease God and oppose everyone by hindering us from speaking to the nations so that they may be saved. Thus they have constantly been filling up the measure of their sins; but God's wrath has overtaken them at last.

But apart from encouragement and warning against Jews, the main point of writing seems to have been uncertainty among the Thessalonians (as surely elsewhere, too) about the return of the 'Lord Jesus Christ'.

'Lord Jesus Christ' the Saviour

The way in which Jesus is referred to throughout the New Testament is interesting, because puzzling. 'Lord', used in the Greek-speaking world as a polite form of address, is regularly used of God in the Greek Jewish scriptures, and in the New Testament it denominates Jesus as divine. 'Christos' is a literal translation, used in the Greek scriptures, of the Hebrew *mashiah*, 'anointed' or 'smeared', indicating a divine appointment to royal or priestly office. It came to be a title for a final deliverer of the Jews. But by Paul and other New Testament writers it is used as part of a name, rather than meaning 'Messiah'. No Greek speaker unfamiliar with the Jewish scriptures would understand it. Nor is it clear in what sense Jesus is understood to fulfil such a role, being no deliverer of the Jews. Heavenly deliverers such as Michael (in Daniel) or Melchizedek (in a few Dead Sea scrolls) are not called 'messiahs'. The name 'Christ' may imply some kind of saving function, but from what? The 'salvation' of Jesus Christ is radically redefined to mean existential rescue from sin and death. For philosophically-minded Greeks, death freed the immortal soul from the perishable body, but the ancient cults of deities such as Dionysus, Osiris and Tammuz, which became popular in the Greek world, seem to have celebrated their revivification from death—symbolic of the vegetation cycle—and this kind of popular cult would have assisted receptivity to the Christian gospel. That most Jews would have understood 'law' as 'enslaving them to sin' (in the singular) and thus death is very doubtful, like their recognition of Jesus Christ as any kind of 'messiah'.

The chief worry of the Thessalonian Christians was Jesus's return. Part of the earliest preaching must have been that he would soon be back, bringing judgment. By the time the Gospel of Matthew was written (ca. 90 CE), this hope remained but had become less immediate (Matthew 24:36-40):

But about that day and hour no one knows, neither the angels of heaven, nor the Son, but only the Father. For as the days of Noah were, so will be the coming of the Son of Man. For as in those days before the flood they were eating and drinking, marrying and giving in marriage, until the day Noah entered the ark, and they knew nothing until the flood came and swept them all away, so too will be the coming of the Son of Man.

A generation after Jesus's earthly life, many Christians had died without seeing his glorious return. Where did that leave them? Paul's response was (1 Thessalonians 4:16-17):

For the Lord himself, with a cry of command, with the archangel's call and with the sound of God's trumpet, will descend from heaven, and the dead in Christ will rise first. Then we who are alive, who are left, will be caught up in the clouds together with them to meet the Lord in the air; and so we will be with the Lord forever.

This is what some evangelicals call the 'Rapture' and are still waiting for. Paul warns against speculating when this will be, while urging his readers to be ready for it (not an easy combination). This means living a 'holy' life and avoiding the morally dubious behaviour that some religious cults permitted.

In his second letter to the Thessalonians, this message is repeated thus (1:6-10):

For it is indeed just of God to repay with affliction those who afflict you, and to give relief to the afflicted as well as to us, when the Lord Jesus is revealed from heaven with his mighty angels in flaming fire, inflicting vengeance on those who do not know God and on those who do not obey the gospel of our Lord Jesus. These will suffer the punishment of eternal destruction, separated from the presence of the Lord and from the glory of his might.

But a complication is now added—Satan (2:7-11):

> For the mystery of lawlessness is already at work, but only until the one who
> now restrains it is removed. And then the lawless one will be revealed, whom
> the Lord Jesus will destroy with the breath of his mouth, annihilating him by
> the manifestation of his coming. The coming of the lawless one is apparent
> in the working of Satan, who uses all power, signs, lying wonders, and every
> kind of wicked deception for those who are perishing, because they refused
> to love the truth and so be saved. For this reason, God sends them a powerful
> delusion, leading them to believe what is false.

Here is the difference from 1 Thessalonians that arouses doubt about
its authenticity: the evil in the world caused by Satan, which God apparently for the moment permits. As described earlier, this was a strand of
Jewish belief about the source of evil. But it complicates Paul's message
considerably.

To the church(es) in Galatia (date uncertain)

In the province of Galatia, Paul's teaching seems to have been widely
repudiated under the influence of what he calls 'Judaizers'. So, two things
had to be stressed: that the Jewish laws are *not* all binding on non-Jewish
Christians, and that Paul's own authority is to be respected. Paul appeals
to his own commission from Jesus and the agreement made in Jerusalem
about non-Jewish membership in the church. By a reverse logic, he argues
that the law must therefore have been valid only until the coming of Jesus,
after which time, it was replaced by the Holy Spirit. The letter also accuses
Peter of reneging on the agreement about sharing meals.

Paul reasserts passionately that the law is now defunct, for Jew and non-
Jew alike. He goes further: if you let yourself be circumcised, you are bound
by the law and have cut yourselves off from Christ. We would surely like
to ask why Paul's own circumcision did not cut him off and learn whether
he himself felt no longer bound to it, in which case he had renounced his
Judaism. His answer may be in 1 Corinthians 9:20: 'to the Jews I was a Jew,
that I might gain the Jews; to those under the law, as under the law, that I
might gain those that are under the law.' Otherwise, then, he was no longer
a Jew?

Finally, there is a passage in this letter that betrays another author
(Galatians 2:7-8): 'for he who worked through Peter making him an apostle to the circumcised also worked through me in sending me to the
Gentiles'. It sounds absolutely authentic, but everywhere else Paul calls
this man 'Cephas' (the Aramaic equivalent of 'Peter', 'rock': See John 1:42).

In Galatians 6:11, Paul writes 'look at the large letters—I am writing this myself.' But not these words. And this claim would not be valid for the many copies that must have been made, either!

To the church in Corinth (various dates)

Two letters to the Corinthians have been preserved, but there is reference to at least one more (1 Corinthians 5:9; 2 Corinthians 2:3). Many scholars conclude that one or both of these preserved letters consists of fragments from other letters. In the first letter, sent from Ephesus (and thus in 53 or 54 CE), Paul shows particular concern, having heard from one group (1 Corinthians 1:11) of division into factions and of dubious moral practices. So, he warns against both. But there seem to have been many specific questions also asked. Paul says that when he 'planted' this community, he fed them 'like babies' with 'milk', since when they have been further instructed by Apollos and by Timothy, whom Paul later sent.

Social as well as doctrinal differences are clearly present, with Jew and non-Jew, poor and rich apparently maintaining their differences, so Paul stresses the unity and equality that ought to exist. Relations within marriages are also addressed. He is not against divorce or remarriage in principle, but does not encourage either. As for practice, the eating of meat offered to 'idols' (the norm in Greco-Roman society, anathema to Jews) is another issue troubling the Corinthians. But it is here that Paul claims he is 'all things to everyone'—a Jew to Jews, a non-Jew to non-Jews, poor to the poor. Is it possible that this declaration is really (despite what has been said to the Galatians) ad hoc and practical, intended only to maintain a community made up from different social circles and who are unable or unwilling to embrace equality?

Paul also takes it upon himself to dictate behavioural norms that are probably simply Jewish. Competitive 'speaking in tongues' is discouraged. Women should either cut their hair short or wear veils, but men leave their heads uncovered since (11:7) they are the image and reflection of God, while women are the reflection of men—and he continues for a while on the subject of female subordination. Even if he is here addressing a specific community whose members have been brought up with different values and habits, and not necessarily legislating for all times and places, this letter is now canonical. Yet canon does not equate with 'word of God', as Christian doctrine assumed, and Paul is entitled to become obsolete. The world moves on—as Paul and his converts did not expect.

There were also some in Corinth who apparently denied the resurrection. Paul insists that, in that case, Jesus was not raised and their belief in him is pointless. Then he shows the results of further thinking beyond his statements to the Thessalonians. The righteous—dead and living—will both acquire new, imperishable bodies at the last day, perhaps like the body of Jesus before his return to heaven. But this suggests non-continuity in human identity and raises an obvious query about the necessity of Jesus's empty tomb. Wisely, Paul goes no further, and the letter ends with personal news, encouragement and the promise of a visit.

The second letter refers to an earlier letter that 'grieved' the Corinthians (7:8)—was it 1 Corinthians, or part of it? The tone here is certainly less harsh than the first letter, but Paul still defends his right to speak as he does because of his calling and what he suffers for it.

Paul and Christian baptism

It may be coincidence that Paul writes about baptism to the Corinthians, but perhaps his thinking on this was prompted by his meeting with Apollos (see Chapter 8) who knew only of the baptism of John. Jewish 'baptism' had an essentially purifying function. It was needed in several rituals of purification and was also a rite of initiation of non-Jews into Judaism. John the Baptizer's rite was one of repentance, but similar to initiation, reaffirming commitment. But as part of Christian initiation, the rite carried connotations of admission to Judaism, to which Paul was opposed. He therefore redefined baptism. In Romans, Paul declares that we die and rise 'with Christ', sharing in his passion and resurrection. This was powerful symbolism, divorced from Judaism but striking a chord with those attached to some popular Greek cults.

To the church in Rome (ca. 55 CE?)

In his letter to the Romans, Paul introduces himself to the Roman Christian community that he has not yet visited, but hopes to. Acts reports that the Jews in Rome had not heard of Paul and knew of him only by rumour; their reception was less unfriendly than in other places. Certainly, this letter is also less hostile to Judaism than, say, Galatians. It is less about simple annulment of the law and more positively about the underlying reason: the 'righteousness', or, as we might say, 'integrity' of God, and about its response—faith. Thus, we have here the most developed and positive statement of Paul's thinking on the essence of Christianity. The world is wicked, and even Paul himself feels the impulse to sin. Punishment must follow, but God also wishes to rescue humans from it. The death of Jesus is the act by which this 'salvation' is accomplished and humans are deemed 'righteous'—the condition being 'faith' in response to this divine 'grace'.

Paul's phrase 'sacrifice of atonement' implies that divine anger was appeased by Jesus's death. This formulation is almost certainly inspired by the scriptures, though in the ancient world, appeasing the gods by sacrifice was a universal practice. Paul, like any well-educated Greek speaker, knows a few rhetorical principles. He captures two neat formulas: in dying according to the Law, Jesus abolished it, and the Jews may have rejected Jesus (and thus God) but God has not rejected them.

There is a useful clue to the dissemination of Paul's letters in chapter 16, a series of greetings, some to persons who we would not expect to have been in Rome. It is likely that these resided in places where Paul had actually been—perhaps Ephesus—in which case the names were added to a copy of the letter dispatched to Ephesus. Paul himself may have been pleased enough with his exposition of Christianity to wish it circulated. But while it overflows with strong images and arguments, it remains open to differences of interpretation—as anyone who reads a few of the numerous commentaries on it will quickly learn!

To the church in Philippi

Paul apparently wrote his friendly letter to the Philippians when imprisoned (1:13). He plans to send Timothy to exchange news, 'when I know more about my circumstances'. The mention of an 'imperial guard' points to Caesarea, where (if Acts is correct) Paul was waiting to be sent to Rome. The mention of 'those from Caesar's household' at the end of the letter (4:22) might suggest Rome itself as the place of writing, but these final verses (vv. 21-23) could come from a separate letter. Two points of particular interest are raised here. One is in 2:6-11, which looks like a quotation of a creed: Jesus was God but 'emptied himself' and took on human nature, to the point of dying, for which God exalted him so that all should confess him as Lord. The other is Paul's account of his earlier life (3:4-9): an Israelite from the tribe of Benjamin (the name 'Saul' gives this away), a 'Hebrew of Hebrews', a Pharisee (and so committed to the Mosaic law), and righteous according to his principles, all of which he now regards as 'dung' because his righteousness comes now from the faithfulness of Christ, whose suffering and resurrection he wishes to share. So here is (again?) a definitive rejection of his own Judaism. He encourages the Philippians, who emerge from this as his most treasured church, to imitate him and to beware of other teachers.

To Philemon

His letter to Philemon is the one genuinely personal letter from Paul, written from prison as an 'old man' (Rome or Ephesus?). Paul has become the 'spiritual father' to a Christian slave called Onesimus. His owner, Philemon, is clearly known by Paul, addressed as a 'brother'. Paul now recommends that Onesimus, having been 'useless' to Philemon, is of benefit to them both, and, though wanting to keep him, is sending him back to his owner. The circumstances of this slave's separation from his master are not given: perhaps he ran away (the usual interpretation), but Paul offers to recompense anything that may have been stolen or owed and asks Philemon to treat his slave as a 'dear brother'. Mark and Luke are included in the final greetings.

Why was this letter included in the New Testament? Possibly it circulated as advice on the treatment of slaves who had become Christian, which we can imagine would have been a problem among Christian communities. The letter does not give a specific recommendation for release, but the language 'no longer as a slave, but more than a slave, a dear brother' carries a very strong hint. There is little evidence of Christian masters routinely freeing their Christian slaves, and freeing slaves deprived them of security and sustenance. This is rather about treating them, within the Christian fellowship, as equals.

Deutero-Pauline letters

Paul's writings inspired others to write in his style, with the aim of developing his thoughts to meet new situations. In some cases, this has been done so well that scholars cannot agree over their authenticity. The numerous greetings to and from co-workers reinforce their Pauline credentials, but the interest in discipline and hierarchy suggests a rapidly expanding Christian population and a waning in expectation of Jesus's return. In Colossians and Ephesians, a cosmic dimension to the gospel also becomes more evident, with the realization that the new cult was now engaged in defining its gospel less within the context of Judaism and its scriptures than the Roman Empire. A cosmic dimension to the status of the risen Jesus emerges, including his victory over the spiritual powers to whom many Christians had previously believed themselves subject.

The two letters to Timothy and the one to Titus fall into a special category. The letters (known as the 'pastoral epistles') were hardly composed for the named addressees, but for wider consumption, following a convention well-known in modern as well as ancient times—though Paul himself wrote for specific recipients. These 'pastoral' letters display an overall concern for order, good public relations, and especially for the offices of *episkopos* ('overseer', later 'bishop') and *diakonos* ('administrator', later 'deacon'). Such concerns are uncharacteristic of Paul and imply a later stage in the organization of Christian communities. The tone here is also rather impersonal and even strict, with specific practical advice given. Prayers and thanks should be offered for the secular authorities; an *episkopos* should have only one wife (Titus 1:6; 1 Timothy 3:2—forbidding polygamy, or divorce, or both?). Women should be subservient to their husbands: none should 'teach or have authority over men'. Various social categories, such as widows, the old, the young and the rich, are also told how to behave. Some of this echoes Paul's instruction to the Corinthians but also illustrates how, as Christian communities grew, spontaneity and variety had to give way to disciplinary structures and formalized codes of behaviour. We might say that the 'spirit' seems to be already giving way to the 'letter'.

The letter to the church in *Colossae,* which Paul seems not to have visited, includes expressions of encouragement and rehearses the struggles that Paul has cheerfully undergone. While these topics resemble those of Paul's genuine letters, the language and style raise doubts about his authorship. There are many words that appear nowhere else in Paul's writings, and the tone seems uncharacteristically formal. The treatment of some themes, such as Jesus's nature and the end of the world, also varies from Paul's genuine writings.

There are also warnings against 'false teachings', including the worship of 'principalities and powers' that rule the earth, and the issue of circumcision is also addressed. Concerning the first, the letter declares that it is Christ who reigns over the entire creation. These powers exist but have been captured through his death. The recipients must put to death the evils of their former ways, since they have become 'new' persons. Circumcision also remained an issue, not for Paul's reasons but because while Judaism was a 'lawful religion' in the empire, avoiding the emperor cult (and other cults) while not being circumcised could lead to discrimination and even persecution. The injunctions to wives to submit to husbands, children to their parents, and slaves to masters reiterates what Paul himself wrote. But in a later context such subordination may also be a deliberate undergirding of the formal hierarchy emerging within the churches.

The letter to the *Ephesians* was probably also aimed at more than one community. It is a plea for unity of the church, as a body of which Christ is the head, enthroned as he is in the 'heavenlies' above all other cosmic powers. The imagery of death followed by life is used more than once and in varied ways. Paul's sufferings and his claim to authority are reasserted, and he speaks as a 'prisoner' (whether in reality or as a metaphor). Ephesians also introduces the notion of Jesus's descent after his death to the 'lower parts of the earth', the abode of the dead in Jewish (and Greek) thought. The reassertion that wives must be subject to husbands might suggest that Christian women were inclined to assert that in Christ all humans were equal, which was clearly unacceptable!

Hebrews

The letter to the Hebrews, despite what some bibles print, does not explicitly claim to be by Paul, and no serious scholar thinks it was. But the final greeting, mentioning 'our brother Timothy', offers a strong hint. Like the other pseudo-Paulines, it has no particular church in mind and its given name probably reflects its profound engagement with the Jewish scriptures. It implies a Jewish authorship, too, beginning 'long ago God spoke to *our* ancestors in many and various ways by the prophets'. The letter proposes the unusual profile of Jesus as a priest, not from the tribe of Levi, but 'of the order of Melchizedek', a mysterious 'king of Salem' in Genesis 14:18, who 'brought out bread and wine' and blessed Abraham. In Psalm 110 (interpreted by Christians as addressed to Jesus), God declares 'Sit at my right hand until I make your enemies your footstool' and 'You are a priest forever according to the order of Melchizedek'. This heavenly priest-king also appears in the Dead Sea Scrolls as the agent in the final redemption of Israel, performing on the Day of Atonement in the final year of world history.

So, as in Paul's letters, Jesus fulfils the law and so frees humans from it, but in a precise cultic manner. Annually, on the Day of Atonement (Leviticus 16), the high priest performed an atoning sacrifice on behalf of all Israel. Jesus, by acting as both priest and victim, has accomplished such a sacrifice to end all sacrifices. Interestingly, there are echoes of the Day of Atonement ritual in the gospel accounts, too: the parting of the curtain in front of the 'holy of holies', the innermost shrine; at Jesus's death, the choice of two victims—Jesus and Barabbas. The mocking and procession to Golgotha may also allude to contemporary celebration of this ritual, as the rabbinic Mishnah describes it. Very possibly, the Melchizedek-Jesus typology shares a common origin with the scroll from Qumran.

This writer, probably a Jew like Paul, stresses continuity rather than disjunction. Chapter 11 lists scriptural examples, beginning with Abel but including many anonymous Jewish men and women, who had faith, that is, who believed in the coming of Jesus before they could see it. In so many ways this letter follows a path parallel to Paul's, but one he would not take. It shows that the gospel did not necessarily entail rejection of Judaism, and for this reason alone deserves as much attention as the works of Paul.

The 'Catholic Epistles'

The 'Catholic Epistles' is the name given to the letters of Peter, John, James and Jude because they seem to be addressed to all the Christian churches. Although relatively disregarded by Bible readers through the ages, these are, like Hebrews, important for attesting strands of early Christianity different from Paul's, in one case blatantly contradicting him. They are quite important, therefore, to the historian of early Christianity if less so to the theologian.

The text of 1 Peter is unlikely to be from the apostle, though it includes the phrase (5:13) 'Your sister church in Babylon, chosen together with you, sends you greetings; and so does my son Mark', with 'Babylon' standing for Rome (as in Revelation). But the Greek is surely too elegant for an Aramaic-speaking Galilean fisherman, and although one could suggest a ghost-writer, there are none of the expected personal reminiscences of Jesus. The usual greetings, Old Testament references, and advice on good Christian behaviour (slaves, wives, etc., all obedient) are present. The writer mentions sufferings to be borne 'for a short time', which will prove the character of the believers: a 'trial of fire' is mentioned, implying that Christians are already being harassed as well as maligned. The message for them is to live orderly and upright lives, and be seen to do so. The 'crown of glory' will be won when the 'chief shepherd' returns.

The text of 2 Peter also claims to be from the apostle, but most scholars think this unlikely too, and doubts circulated even in the early Christian centuries. Although there are now references to some of the apostle's experiences at Jesus's baptism and at his transfiguration, and to Jesus's imminent death, the letter, stylistically different from 1 Peter, borrows from the letter of Jude and seems to know some of 'our dear brother' Paul's letters. It also contains an interesting allusion to the myth in Enoch of angelic 'sinners' who were 'thrown into hell' to be kept until the day of judgment. Similar divine punishments await the 'false teachers', on whom the letter spends a lot of time. That judgment will come soon, writes the author, amid cosmic upheaval. But in criticizing false teaching and explaining the delayed coming of Jesus as offering more people the opportunity for salvation, this letter clearly reflects a second or even third generation of Christian believers.

The letters of John are probably from one author, who calls himself the 'Elder'. Only the second and third of these actually take the form of a letter, and both are very brief. The second is addressed to a 'dear lady' and her children, maybe suggesting a 'mother' church with 'daughter' communities. The first letter, longer and more formal, refers to 'deceivers' who have left the church, whose own beliefs are unclear, and also to visiting 'prophets', against whom love will overcome dissension. Like the gospel, it makes a point of the author's personal testimony to Jesus and contrasts the light that Jesus brings with the darkness of the world. The third letter is written to a Gaius, probably concerning this same church as in the second letter, and concerning a Diotrephes who is rejecting the writer's authority and spreading false charges against him.

The theme of love as a supreme Christian virtue is reminiscent of the Gospel of John, and many scholars have suggested a 'Johannine Christianity' to which the gospel and the letters belong—though not the book of Revelation. If such a form of Christianity existed, it was characterized by an intense devotion to Jesus as divine, a strong antipathy to Judaism, a belief in the possession of 'eternal life' and a tendency to a dualistic outlook on the world. But it will also have suffered internal dissent, as did the Pauline gospel.

The epistle of James offers a stark contrast to both Pauline and Johannine versions of Christianity. It does not even focus on Jesus and its references to 'the Lord' may be to God (the father). Far from attacking Judaism, it emphasizes good works. Indeed, it is one New Testament book with which no Jew could express much disagreement. Addressed to the 'twelve tribes of the Diaspora', it expounds the virtues of patience and humility, control of one's speech (with a fine section on 'the tongue') and support of the poor and weak. In saying 'faith by itself, if it has no works, is dead', the writer seems to rebuke Paul's insistence on 'faith' (we can see why Martin Luther called this an 'epistle of straw'). Whoever the author, this version of the gospel fits the description of the Jerusalem church in Acts, which was led by Jesus's brother, James, explaining the attribution to him.

The author of the epistle of Jude claims the identity of the brother of the disciple James, but, as with Peter, such a man could hardly write in such a good Greek style. Endorsing the teaching of the 'apostles' also hints at a date beyond Jude's own lifetime. With no personal greetings, the writer issues a general warning about false teaching, without identifying it. Like the epistle of James, it does not address the status or nature of Jesus, nor attack Judaism, and the wording of the final blessing to 'God our Saviour, through Jesus Christ our Lord' is worth noting carefully.

Chapter Ten

Revelation: The End of the Story

'The revelation (*apokalypsis*) of Jesus Christ, which God ... made known by sending his angel to his servant John'. This is how the book of Revelation opens, and John later describes himself as an 'elder' living on the island of Patmos. Though popular with several contemporary evangelical Christians, this curious book was only with difficulty accepted in the New Testament canon.

Inspired by several Old Testament writings, especially Daniel, Ezekiel and Zechariah, and possibly based on other lost Jewish apocalypses, Revelation is saturated with symbols. There are, to begin with, letters to seven churches, a scroll with seven seals, seven angels, and seven bowls. The whole book might also be divided into seven parts, though its structure is complicated and seems to consist of successive scenarios that, if taken in sequence, become rather ludicrous. A better explanation is that different reworkings of Daniel (and sometimes Ezekiel)—perhaps even different literary compositions—have been strung together.

The reason for the composition of this elaborate 'vision' has long been held as the outbreak of persecution, usually attributed to the reign of the Roman emperor Domitian (81–96 CE), though Nero (37–68 CE) and Vespasian (69–79 CE) are also contenders. But evidence for systematic persecution in the first century is sparse, and what drives the book's anti-Roman rhetoric may be the newly introduced cult of the deified emperor. Lack of obedience to this cult was a major source of resentment against Christians.

A clearly marked opening section (chapters 1–3) is a series of letters to seven churches in Asia, who are variously judged with regard to their teaching, their attitude towards Judaism, and their degree of persecution and self-satisfaction. The remainder of the book consists of a vision of the heavenly world, revealing what will occur in the near future. Chapters 4–5 describe the throne of God (influenced by Ezekiel 1 and Daniel 7). A scroll fastened with seven seals is produced and it is declared that the 'Lion of the tribe of Judah, from the 'Root of David' is the only one worthy to open it. The 'Lamb' with seven horns and seven eyes takes the scroll. The title 'lamb' echoes John 1, and the horns and eyes feature in Daniel 7. Earthly and heavenly beings praise the Lamb, asserting his cosmic sovereignty (and clearly challenging the Roman emperor's claims).

The seals are then opened in turn, bringing on the 'Four Horsemen of the Apocalypse' (Zechariah 1:8), who wreak terrible judgment on the earth. The opening of the fifth seal reveals the souls of martyrs, and the sixth the 'wrath of the Lamb', announced by an earthquake, falling stars and a receding sky. Before the climax of the seventh seal, 144,000 of the 'tribes of Israel' receive a seal on their foreheads (Revelation 7:3-4). Before the throne of God stand the many who 'come out of the great tribulation', clothed with robes 'made white in the blood of the Lamb'.

At the opening of the seventh seal, seven angels receive seven trumpets, while an eighth takes a golden censer filled with fire and throws it to the earth, causing peals of thunder, rumblings, flashes of lightning, and an earthquake. At each trumpet blast something happens: a star falls from the sky, it is given the key to hell, it opens up, smoke rises and darkens the earth, a swarm of locusts appears with human hair and faces and lions' teeth (Daniel 7). At the sixth trumpet, four angels 'bound at the river Euphrates' are freed to prepare two hundred million horsemen, who kill a third of mankind by plagues of fire, smoke and brimstone. But the rest of humanity does not repent.

In chapter 10, an angel appears with a small scroll open in his hand. Seven thunderclaps utter mysteries and secrets, which John is commanded not to write down. Rather, he is to eat the scroll (Ezekiel 3). The idea conveyed here is of 'swallowed secrets', to be revealed only at a later time, and/ or to a chosen few. Then, still following Ezekiel, we are given a description of the 'new Jerusalem'. John receives a rod to measure the temple, whose courts are trodden by the nations for three and a half years (Daniel 12:7). Two witnesses prophesy for 1,260 days (compare Daniel 12:11-12), clothed in sackcloth (a sign of mourning). Seven bowls, full of God's wrath, are then distributed to be poured out. The heavenly temple opens and the ark of the covenant is seen. More thunder and lightning, earthquake, and hail.

Now a new scenario is introduced: a woman in a white robe, with the sun at her back, the moon under her feet, and on her head a crown of twelve stars. She is pregnant with a son. A dragon with seven heads, ten horns, and seven crowns drags a third of the stars of heaven with his tail, and throws them to the earth (Daniel 7 again). The dragon waits for the birth of the child so he can devour it. But when the child is born, he is caught up to God's throne while the woman flees into the wilderness. War breaks out in heaven between Michael and the dragon (the Devil, Satan: 12:9). The dragon and his angels are defeated and cast out of Heaven for good. The dragon aims to persecute the woman, but she is helped to escape, enraging the dragon into waging war against the rest of her offspring, who 'keep the commandments of God and hold the testimony of Jesus' (12:17).

Another figure, a beast with seven heads, ten horns, and ten crowns on his horns, emerges from the sea (Daniel 7:2-3). The people of the world follow this beast, whom the dragon grants power and authority for forty-two months (that is, three and a half years again). The beast of the sea wages war against the saints (Daniel 7:21) and overcomes them. Another beast directs people to make an image of the wounded beast of the sea, forcing all people to bear the mark of the beast, which is 666.

The Lamb stands on Mount Zion with the 144,000 redeemed from earth and victorious over the beast. One 'like the Son of Man' reaps the earth. A second angel reaps 'the vine of the earth' and throws it into the great winepress of the wrath of God. The temple of the tabernacle, in heaven, is opened. Seven angels are given a golden bowl, containing the seven last plagues bearing the wrath of God (15:6-8).

Now yet another scenario. The angel who had the seven bowls gives John a vision: the great harlot sitting on a scarlet beast; she is Babylon the Great. Babylon is destroyed and the marriage supper of the Lamb follows, with judgment on the two beasts, the dragon, and the dead (19:11-20:15). The beast and the (recently introduced) false prophet are cast into the lake of fire, the dragon is imprisoned in the bottomless pit for a thousand years (1 Enoch?), the resurrected martyrs live and reign with Christ for a thousand years. But in a kind of coda, after the thousand years, the dragon is released and goes out to deceive the nations in the four corners of the Earth—Gog and Magog (Ezekiel 38–39)—and gathers them for battle at the holy city. The dragon makes war against the people of God, but is defeated and cast into the lake of fire with the beast and the false prophet.

At the last judgment, the wicked, along with Death and Hades, are cast into the lake of fire, the 'second death'. A new, glorious heaven replaces the old earth. There is no more suffering or death. God comes to dwell with humanity in the 'new Jerusalem', which is then described in terms of a new Garden of Eden. The river of life and the tree of life appear for the healing of the nations and peoples. The curse of sin is ended. The book ends with Christ's reassurance that his coming is imminent, and with final admonitions (22:6-21).

Revelation is undoubtedly a dramatic finale to the New Testament story of Jesus and indeed the story of the present world. Rather than try to identify the meaning of the symbols (just a few are easy: the church, the Roman emperor, Satan) or to convert these convoluted images into a kind of science fiction Apocalypse, it is best to try and understand the purpose and the effect of such a piece of work. There are two lines of interpretation that are not mutually exclusive. One is a reworking of the scriptural scenarios of Ezekiel and Daniel into a specifically Christian vision of the end, giving the exalted Jesus a central place. This approach might even allow for several different versions that the author has decided to combine, at the cost of coherence.

The other line of interpretation, which also explains the creation of Daniel, is an experience of events that challenge the essential belief in the ultimate vindication by God of his chosen people. The 'apocalyptic' response is to abandon any sense of an ongoing historical process in favour of a divine script, only now being revealed, in which the growing power of evil precedes a dramatic intervention from God or his agent to finally destroy evil and all its manifestations, human or supernatural.

But whether by design or chance, Revelation supplies an appropriate conclusion to the Christian Bible, as well as to the mission of Jesus and the purposes of God. It mirrors Genesis in undoing creation, bringing together the divided heaven and earth (the first act of creation), and ushering in the paradise that the Garden of Eden had once been. It makes of the Christian Bible a complete cycle, while tying together the two Testaments through its integration of Old Testament (and Jewish) imagination into a Christian vision.

Much may be said against this book, not least its predilection for dualism and violence. But as with all biblical writings, less fault lies with an author than with those readers who fail to do justice to the aim and character of what is written.

Part Four

Philosophy, Ethics and Piety

Chapter Eleven

Divination: Prophecy and Apocalyptic

The authors and readers of both the Old and the New Testaments lived in what is often called a 'prescientific' age, when the factors that determined much of human life—disease, famine, war, childbirth, the weather—were believed to depend on the activity of supernatural agents: gods, demons, spirits. These could be manipulated by various rites of intercession, appeasement or gratitude.

It was important to understand the moods and intentions of these beings, but also to anticipate their actions. This was done in two ways. One was to ask directly, such as by drawing lots. This is how Achan was found out in Joshua 7 and Saul chosen as king in 1 Samuel 10. But divination was usually something a little more 'professional' and 'scientific'. The world was full of mysterious or unusual phenomena (irregular births, eclipses, movements of stars, dreams) that suggested the gods were revealing something. A whole industry grew up, in Mesopotamia especially, with guilds of specialists interpreting 'omens' such as patterns of oil on water, astronomical phenomena, the entrails of sacrificed animals, or dreams. 'Manticism' is the name given to this 'science', and traces are found in the Old Testament (and in the New) in what are called 'apocalypses' or 'revelations'. These traces are a belief that the future is predetermined and thus predictable, and that it is revealed to a 'seer' interpreting signs. Revelation is an apocalypse, and Isaiah, Ezekiel and Daniel contain them, as does 1 Enoch. The star followed by the magi in Matthew hints at the ancient Mesopotamian science of astronomical symbolism. An apocalypse can be hard to distinguish formally from a prophetic vision but the crucial criterion is a fixed and predetermined divine plan (apocalyptic) or a flexible divine response (prophecy).

But (apart from the rare use of lots) divination is represented in the Old Testament by 'prophecy'. Scriptural prophecy is a creation of the 'Deuteronomic' theology that also created the books of Kings, that is, it implies a written covenant and its law. Deuteronomic theology holds that signs cannot be coerced from its god: he will deliver his messages as he chooses and only through words or visions. He does not know or plan the future exactly, since that is subject to the terms of the covenant (in Deuteronomy). The future depends on Israel's behaviour, and prophets are needed for words of encouragement or warning. The presentation of an institution or office, of a 'succession of prophets', is an important but fictitious element of the Deuteronomic philosophy of history.

According to Deuteronomy, the true prophet must speak what Yahweh has told him, his prophecy must come true, and what he says must not contradict Yahweh's revealed law. These conditions may at first seem ridiculous: the inability of the people to recognize a true prophet until afterwards, and the inability of the prophet to tell people what they do not already know (or should know). But they are logical. The one great 'prophecy' is the law, and the supreme prophet is Moses. Contemporary prophets represent a dangerous challenge to the law, and so they become valid only retrospectively, as upholders of the law and accurate predictors of the future. In the *present*, one should not heed *any* prophet.

PROPHECY IN THE NEW TESTAMENT

'Prophet' was a term used within the Judaism of Jesus's day to describe any religious leader outside the priestly or scribal establishment. John the Baptizer and Jesus are both so described. The New Testament has a fairly clear perception of its significance. Acts 2:17-18 quotes Joel 2:28:

> In the last days it will be, God declares,
> that I will pour out my Spirit upon all flesh,
> and your sons and your daughters shall prophesy,
> and your young men shall see visions,
> and your old men shall dream dreams,
> my slaves, men and women,
> in those days I will pour out my Spirit;
> and they shall prophesy.

Like the Old Testament, the New understands prophecy as a gift of the spirit, but now available to all. In Paul's view, it is different from the gift of 'speaking in tongues': 'For those who speak in a tongue do not speak to other people but to God; for nobody understands them, since they are speaking mysteries in the Spirit. On the other hand, those who prophesy

speak to other people for their upbuilding and encouragement and conso-
lation' (1 Corinthians 14:2). Revelation describes itself as 'prophecy', probably both in the Pauline sense of encouragement and also as prediction. But
what is there now to predict? We can guess that other Christian prophets
offered their encouragement by depicting the imminent climax to the history of the world. There are references in the gospels and letters to 'false
prophets' too, who will lead believers astray. Presumably 'false prophecy'
was a useful charge to level against teachers of alternative opinions.

THE PROPHETIC 'MESSAGE'

The prophetic books were not transmitted verbatim by disciples. That
there is very little biographical detail concerning the 'minor prophets'
tells against this conclusion. Analysis of the books themselves suggests a
lengthy and elaborate process in which 'messages' are updated to address
later times. The books may present themselves as issuing a 'message'
appropriate to their own times, but the majority reflect 'messages' for different contexts.

There is little doubt that the prophetic books do include genuine
material from persons who, officially or unofficially, recorded what they
claimed were messages from God. Parallels to these messages from elsewhere, including Assyria, suggest that, whether spoken or not, they were
written and were archived in the palace or among temple scribes. Many of
these communications are introduced by the words 'Thus says Yahweh',
adopting the formula used by messengers. Correspondence was sometimes
carried out by means of written letters, but also by word of mouth. Then a
messenger was needed to recite the words exactly as dictated. When David
wishes to communicate with his general Joab (2 Samuel 11:25):

> David said to the messenger, "Thus you shall say to Joab, 'Do not let this
> matter trouble you...

'Thus you shall say' introduces the precise text of the message, like quotation marks. When the messenger delivers his message, he starts 'thus
says...' and then offers the message verbatim.

The formula shows a prophet literally quoting a verbal letter from the
deity. But the prophet did not carry any reply back and, in a further difference, sometimes commented on the message with his own words. He
might even start with them. Or the author may intrude by writing: 'the
word of Yahweh came to so-and-so, saying...'. It can then become hard, if

not impossible, to tell which words are supposedly coming from the writer, the prophet, or God. Jeremiah chapter 11 is a good example.

The recipient of the prophet's message is not always clear. Sometimes we get an explicit address: a city, 'people of Jerusalem', or 'children of Israel', as if the message is declared publicly, which may have been the case. But what about threats against foreign nations? Were they really recited in Moab or Babylon or Tyre? And what is their point, anyway, unless for local consumption, announcing that the god of Israel is the god of all nations, who has messages for them, too—and can deal with any trouble they cause.

Other prophetic forms of speech include laments (from mourning festivals), accusations (from legal disputes), and curses. Mostly these are in poetry, suggesting they were composed for reciting publicly. Another prophetic device is the vision. When Amos sees a basket of summer fruit (Amos 8:2), or Jeremiah the branch of an almond tree (Jeremiah 1:11), they talk of being 'shown' it, as if their eyes are divinely directed. The message is then a wordplay. 'Summer' can also mean 'end' and 'almond' can mean 'watch over'. More elaborate is Ezekiel's vision of a valley of dry bones (chapter 37) or of a final battle with Gog of Magog (38–39). The meaning of these visions is not spelt out, but is presumably metaphorical. Like Ezekiel, Zechariah also contains some quite elaborate visions of the future, some of which are updated in the book of Revelation.

The visions in Daniel sit firmly within an apocalyptic (mantic) conceptual framework of a preordained end to a divine historical plan. Daniel is given the interpretation to the visions of others; later, his own visions are explained to him by an angel. The mantic seer, unlike the prophet, is not so much the recipient of a sign, but of its *interpretation*, a sign, like the inspector of animal entrails or the stargazer.

Do these messages reproduce actual experiences, or are they invented as an effective way of conveying a message? There is evidence that prophets underwent ecstatic experiences (1 Samuel 19:20), possibly deliberately induced (2 Kings 3:15), but this hardly answers the question! Elaborate apocalypses like Revelation, or those of Enoch or Daniel, look like literary constructions, especially when they correlate closely with historical events, when we may suspect they were composed *after* the events they are supposed to predict.

Finally, let's not ignore prophetic actions. Isaiah (20:2-5) walks about naked, Jeremiah (13:1-11) hides a loincloth by the Euphrates, and Ezekiel (3:1-3) eats a scroll. Whether these signs were performed must also be doubtful; they are often highly improbable stories told to dramatize the message, rather like parables.

COMPOSITION OF THE PROPHETIC BOOKS

The focus of the prophetic books is mainly Jerusalem, the object of divine threat and promise and the symbol of the future. This is an important clue to the process by which these writings accumulated. Mostly they did not grow organically: they have (Jonah excepted) no narrative, plot or easily recognizable structure. There are signs of editorial organization, but they still resemble *anthologies* most of all. The following summaries present the major features and issues concerning the origin and growth of each book.

Most books open with a dating formula by the reigns of the kings of Judah and Israel (or of Persia). This correlation of rulers is also characteristic of the books of Kings, with which both Isaiah and Jeremiah share some pieces of narrative (2 Kings 18:14-20:19 = Isaiah 36:1-39:8 and 2 Kings 24:18-25:30 = Jeremiah 52:1-34). The editing of the 'minor prophets' as well as of Jeremiah can in fact be assigned to the same circles as the compilers of Kings, the 'Deuteronomists'. The Major Prophets (Isaiah, Jeremiah, Ezekiel) cluster round the same historical moment—the destruction of Jerusalem at the beginning of the sixth century. In biblical historiography, this moment marks the end of the 'old Israel' and the birth of new ones (as we have seen above).

ISAIAH

Isaiah, the largest prophetic book and the first in canonical order and chronological setting, features a prophet from the middle of the eighth century who was closely involved in Jerusalem politics and particularly with the kings Ahaz and Hezekiah (740–690). It was during this time that the kingdom of Israel ended (722). Much of chapters 1–39 is consistent with that period, but 40–55 presuppose the sixth century, when the Persian king, Cyrus, permitted deportees to return to their homelands. Biblical scholars thus refer to 'First Isaiah' (1–39) and 'Second Isaiah' (40–55), and even recognize a 'Third Isaiah' in chapters 56-66. The later sections were not simply added on to a completed First Isaiah: it seems that the compiler of 40–55 incorporated a collection of earlier Isaiah texts and prefaced them to his own writing, creating the first draft of the canonized book. But a lot of additional editing also took place afterwards.

Jerusalem (often called 'Zion') is the obvious theme of the Isaiah collection. In chapter 6, Isaiah has a vision of 'Yahweh of Hosts' (his characteristic title) in the Jerusalem temple, surrounded by seraphim crying 'holy,

holy, holy' (another favourite divine title is 'Holy One of Israel'). Among criticisms of wickedness and threats of disaster, the prophet urges the king and people to trust in the god of Jerusalem and not in foreign alliances. In 40–55, so-called 'Third Isaiah', which presupposes the ruin of the city, a new life is offered with the return of the children of the city to their mother. Those 'children' are encouraged with the hope of better things, but a critical tone is also introduced: present sufferings are due to short-comings. Both Second and Third Isaiah imagine Jerusalem as a future place of pilgrimage for people of many lands, recognizing its god as universal.

The book, as a whole, turns on the narrative of chapters 36–39, relating how an Assyrian siege of Jerusalem failed, as the god of Jerusalem showed his power to defend it. But the story ends with king Hezekiah welcoming envoys of the Babylonian king and showing them his treasures, prompting Isaiah's prediction that his descendants will one day be taken away and become servants of the Babylonian king. This warning sets the scene for Second Isaiah, which celebrates a second divine intervention in favour of Jerusalem—the return of its lost inhabitants.

In Christian interpretation, Isaiah is celebrated less for its interest in Zion than for messianic predictions. The most famous of these is in 7:14: 'behold, a young woman [translated into Greek as 'virgin'] shall conceive and bear a son, and you shall call his name "Immanuel"'. Near the begin-ning of Second Isaiah (40:3) is the call 'A voice crying, "In the wilderness prepare the way of Yahweh"', with which Matthew, Mark and Luke intro-duce John the Baptist. In Second Isaiah, we also find a group of poems called the 'Servant Songs', in which an unidentified figure suffers for the sins of others: he is 'despised and rejected'; he 'bears our grief and carries our sorrows'; he is 'brought as a lamb to slaughter'; God makes his soul an 'offering for sin'. These words feed the gospels' description of Jesus's death, but the historical identity of this 'servant' (or perhaps 'servants'?) remains disputed: in at least one case he is named as 'Israel', perhaps the deportees who bore the punishment for the sins of the whole people.

A secondary theme in Isaiah 40–55 is condemnation of divine images. Because these chapters were once thought to have been written in Babylonia, such criticism was taken to refer to the dangers of idolatry there. But Judah is now being seen as a more probable context, suggesting rather a ban on images of Yahweh, as expressed in the Ten Commandments. This is accompanied by a strong affirmation that Yahweh is the only god, creator of light and darkness, of good and evil, as 45:7 puts it.

Third Isaiah (specifically chapter 61) introduces a divinely-appointed messenger: 'The spirit of the Lord Yahweh is upon me, because Yahweh has anointed me...', which is quoted in Luke 4, when Jesus is given the scroll to read in the synagogue, and adds 'Today, the scripture has been fulfilled in your hearing'. This and other texts explain why Isaiah has been called the 'Fifth Gospel', but the messianic theme only covers a small part of the contents. Indeed, the book covers many topics: in 13–23 is a large collection of oracles against foreign nations, yet Second and Third Isaiah seem to advocate a temple of Yahweh open to all nations. A book whose composition spans many centuries will of course reflect different historical and theological contexts, not just the 'message' of a single prophet.

JEREMIAH

The canonized Hebrew edition of Jeremiah (found in nearly all modern bibles), was not used in the earliest Christian bibles, whose Greek text was translated from a different edition that has now turned up among the Dead Sea Scrolls. It is about 15% shorter, though the differences do not greatly affect the meaning. One exception is that the longer edition calls Jeremiah 'the prophet' 26 times, while the shorter Greek edition does so only four times. That difference points to some deliberate, tendentious editing.

Like Isaiah, Jeremiah appears in a time of crisis for Jerusalem, and, like Isaiah (probably) and Ezekiel (certainly), he was a priest. His pronouncements are dated from the thirteenth year of King Josiah (ca. 640–609) until just after the destruction of Jerusalem in 586. One unique feature is the presence of a scribe, Baruch, who, chapter 36 relates, copied all of Jeremiah's words onto a scroll, which the king burnt and which was later replaced by a fuller version.

This book shows best of all how the profile of a prophet can be radically changed as different ideologies and interests direct its editing. The Benjaminite prophet came under the protection of the family of Gedaliah, the later ruler of Judah in Mizpah, where the earliest written collection of Jeremiah's words presumably originated. His criticisms would underline how the god of Jerusalem had given up on both the royal house and the temple, implying divine support for the new regime. Chapters 1–25 reflect this historical setting and include messages for all or some of the people of Samaria, who are addressed as 'house of Israel'. Thus, the new regime may have recognized Samarians as Israelites and even brothers. A letter for the Judahite deportees in chapter 29 also fits this context: it tells them to settle down in Babylonia, suggesting that Jeremiah and his patrons had no wish to see the old regime return.

But the letter has been updated to reflect a contrary view! 'When Babylon's seventy years are completed', it continues, God will bring the Judahite establishment back, a message reinforced in chapter 30. Chapters 50–51 are explicitly anti-Babylonian and pro-Jerusalem: 'Yahweh of Hosts, the Holy One of Israel' (titles from the old Jerusalem cult, used by Isaiah) will punish Babylon and destroy it. Jeremiah is now concerned with Jerusalem's restoration. But chapter 31 contains promises of restoration to Israel/Samaria and to Judah, and though it does not anticipate a reunification, there is clearly a single religious community envisaged. The verse most quoted by Christian readers (v. 31) runs: 'The days are surely coming, says Yahweh, when I will make a new covenant with the house of Israel and the house of Judah'. The 'new covenant' is echoed in Jesus's words at the Last Supper, making Jeremiah, like Isaiah, a prophet of the gospel.

Chapters 26–29 relate conflicts with 'false prophets', in which Jeremiah is sometimes accuser and sometimes accused. This conflict may well have a historical basis and certainly provides a possible reason why 'the prophet' was so often added to his name in the longer edition of the book. One more major component is a series of 'Confessions' (11–12, 15, 17, 18 and 20), where Jeremiah complains to his god about being commanded to pronounce such hard words, and about the resulting persecution he faces. Do these uniquely reveal the inner turmoil of the historical prophet? There is no way to tell, but they are fairly standard, stylized and stereotyped, like several of the Psalms, and were very likely added later to help convert Jeremiah from an enthusiastic anti-Jerusalem prophet into a reluctant one.

Jeremiah is also converted into a great supporter of Deuteronomy. Alongside the poetic utterances are prose narratives (26–29, 32, 34–44) with a pronounced Deuteronomistic style. Chapter 25, for example, reviews Judah's history of rejecting 'my servants the prophets' and not 'turning from your evil way' in the land that Yahweh 'gave to the ancestors'. Few scholars assign these to a historical Jeremiah.

The book ends with a narrative of Gedaliah assassinated and the population fleeing, mostly to Egypt, with Jeremiah among them. This is commonly accepted as a historical fact, but the point of this story is to move the population conveniently out of the way, so that Judah could be 'empty' for the returning Judahites from Babylonia. So such a flight from Judah remains unproven.

LAMENTATIONS

Lamentations is the first of three books associated with Jeremiah in the Old Testament (but not in the Hebrew scriptures). The ascriptions are, however, fanciful. Lamentations is a collection of bitter reflections on the fall of Jerusalem. The interesting feature of this collection is the different perspective of each lament, ranging from sorrow, through contrition to protest. Such responses echo the ambiguity of the Old Testament over the punishment of exile: inflicted on the guilty but borne by the innocent. Second Isaiah seems to represent the returning Judahites as having suffered for others (their ancestors), while Jeremiah (31:29) and Ezekiel (18:2) both quote 'the parents have eaten sour grapes and the children's teeth are set on edge'. The 'restored' Israels of Ezra and Nehemiah, too, faced the dilemma of reclaiming an ancestry while repudiating its disobedience. Such ambivalence resounds throughout the prophetic books as they mix condemnation of the past and present with hope for the future. Indeed, if we had to give just one reason for the prophetic collection, it would be this: the past was bad but taught the lesson that the future will be better.

BARUCH AND THE LETTER OF JEREMIAH

The apocryphal works (non-existent in Hebrew) of Baruch and the Letter of Jeremiah are sometimes put together in modern bibles. Baruch (or 1 Baruch) claims to have been written by Jeremiah's scribe in Babylon (though Jeremiah was never there). It asks the Jerusalemites to pray for the Babylonian king and expresses repentance for the ancestors' sins, while expressing hope for restoration. In imagery reminiscent of Second Isaiah, the Jerusalem of the future is seen welcoming back returnees from all lands. The Letter of Jeremiah is concerned (again like Second Isaiah) with idols, a topic absent from the book of Jeremiah itself.

EZEKIEL

The career of Ezekiel, the strangest of the Major Prophets, is precisely dated, suggesting (but perhaps wrongly) a real historical personage. Ezekiel begins (1:1-3) among the deportees in Babylonia, where the 'hand of Yahweh' and the 'word of Yahweh' came upon him. He has a startling vision of heaven, with angelic beings alongside a wheeled throne bearing a humanlike figure, the 'appearance of the glory of Yahweh'. The wheels mean that Yahweh is not tied to Jerusalem but can move in any imaginable direction, and chapters 8–11 show him leaving the Jerusalem temple because of its corruption (possibly going to Babylonia). The voice from the throne commissions Ezekiel as a prophet, addressing him—as throughout the book—as 'son of man', an important title in the New Testament, but of uncertain significance here. He is shown a scroll and told to eat it. Weird visions and actions continue to characterize the book.

A major puzzle is the division of Ezekiel's activity between Babylonia and Judah. Ostensibly, he begins his prophetic work in Babylonia, and is carried 'by the spirit' back to Judah. But there is evidence of an interest in events before he was deported, so perhaps his career actually began earlier. Chapters 1–24 contain prophecies against Judah and Jerusalem, and seem best to fall before his deportation. These are followed by a block of oracles against foreign nations (chapters 25–32), which give way to optimistic oracles about the future, when a new city and temple will be built and all twelve tribes of Israel will again live in a renovated land. Among the vivid visions of the future are the 'valley of dry bones' (chapter 37), the great battle with the mysterious Gog of Magog (38–39), and a detailed description of the new temple city. Several of these items are updated in the book of Revelation.

Ezekiel has some stark, even pornographic imagery. Jerusalem is Yahweh's wife, whose adultery will be punished by displaying her nudity in public (chapter 16); Jerusalem and Samaria are depicted as sexually promiscuous daughters (chapter 23). 'Your origin and your birth', he says, 'were in the land of the Canaanites; your father was an Amorite, and your mother a Hittite'. It is doubtful whether the preserved remnant will really be forgiven, for Ezekiel's god is exalted, holy and aloof, acting for the sake of his honour only. The vision for the future is not of a restored nation, but a transformed one, living in reassigned tribal settlements and with a new temple city, not (despite the view of many readers) identified as Jerusalem, and indeed placed in a different location. The inclusion of Samaria in the future Israel is unique among the prophetic books. It is also a most unlikely prospect from a deported Jerusalem priest.

Attempts have been made to psychoanalyse the eccentric individual assumed to be behind the book. But we might well be engaging with an elaborately constructed figure. Why was this very odd prophetic book canonized? Among some circles (the Dead Sea Scrolls and the author of Revelation) it has, nevertheless, been very influential.

THE MINOR PROPHETS

The Hebrew 'Book of the Twelve' becomes in Christian bibles thirteen individual books, and in a slightly different order. Daniel is the extra book, but it is apocalyptic rather than prophetic. We can in most cases assume a historical individual produced some oracles that were assembled, edited and expanded over the following centuries to contribute to an overall 'prophetic' message. But some of the prophets are invented, and all are the outcome of a scribal project based, and sometimes built, on archives of identifiable historical individuals.

Hosea

The prophet Hosea is dated to the first half of the eighth century, and his words contain warnings of doom to Israel and promise to Judah. He is assumed to be an Israelite. The book's most striking feature is its opening, where Hosea is commanded by Yahweh to marry a prostitute, Gomer. She will bear him children named 'Jezreel' (a major royal city), a daughter Lo-Ruhamah ('Pitiless') and a second son 'Lo-Ammi' ('Not my People'). Whether these symbolic actions actually happened or not is hard to decide. Nor does it matter: the purpose is to depict Israel as Yahweh's habitually unfaithful wife and, like Ezekiel, her humiliation is graphically depicted. Baal, the main deity of the Levant, takes the role of boy-friend, a weather-god responsible for the fertility of the land. But for Hosea, it is Yahweh, the husband, who looks after his wife, providing for her wellbeing, as a good husband should.

At the end of the book is a note: 'whoever is wise, let them understand: the ways of Yahweh are right'. This is a clue that the prophetic books were later read by individuals to discern how to follow the divine law. We learn that, whether or not prophets originally declaimed in public, the books named after them were ultimately read by pious Jews—and by Christians, as clues to the life of Jesus: 'Out of Egypt have I called my son' (Hosea 11:1) is quoted in Matthew 2:15.

Joel

Joel is one of several prophets about whom we are told nothing. His name ('Yahweh is god') might suggest an invented identity and his father's name, Pethuel, is strange ('God has deceived'?). Chapter 1 describes a locust plague that destroys all crops, leading to calls for lament: 'the Day of Yahweh is coming!' (1:15). But in chapter 2 the plague becomes a metaphor, and the locust swarm is a human army, raised by Yahweh. So, says the prophet, repent now: fast, weep, wear sackcloth, and maybe Yahweh will relent. And suddenly he does, promising new wine, new grain, new oil. In the best-known saying of the book, Yahweh then promises to 'pour out his spirit on all people'; the old will dream, the young have visions. This verse will be quoted in Acts 2:17 as a prediction of the coming of the Spirit at Pentecost. But no more explanation comes here, only that the day of Yahweh will be dark and dreadful. The nations will be judged for what they have done, and Yahweh calls them to battle, to turn their ploughshares and pruning hooks into weapons. He roars from Zion, and the earth shakes.

How are these contents related? We recognize a promise of vengeance on the nations for what they have done, the restoration of Jerusalem and of the scattered 'Israel' (a clue to the date). But there remains a threat, since 'Israel' has offended. Combining punishment on Israel with punishment on other nations is unusual. And how does a locust plague represent a day of vengeance on other nations? We can speculate that a prophetic warning prompted by a locust plague has been universalized into a final divine punishment on all nations but with a promise of ultimate restoration of 'Israel' (clearly meaning Judah). But the organization of this idea is rather messy.

Amos

Amos's birthplace is given as Tekoa, usually identified as a town of Judah. But, like Hosea, his words mostly address Israel. The contents are better organized than most other books, with groups of sayings combined into units and interspersed with relevant bits of narrative. The book opens with Yahweh 'roaring from Zion' (repeating Joel 3:16), followed by a series of oracles against Israel's neighbours and culminating in one against Israel itself. A relatively weak condemnation of Judah has been attached later. The central chapters condemn hypocrisy, perversion of justice and ill-treatment of the poor, and even claim that Yahweh is not much interested in sacrifices. 'Did you bring to me sacrifices and offerings the forty years in the wilderness, O house of Israel?' (5:25). Israel's special status is also challenged: You Israelites are just like the Ethiopians to me! Did I not bring Israel from Egypt, but also Philistines from Crete and Arameans from Kir? (9:7). The overall message is stark: destruction and deportation (though how this helps the poor is not clear). A final sequence of visions illustrates this fate with increasing force: Yahweh relents his judgment at first, but finally does not, and the temple of Bethel, where Amos is uttering his words, crashes down.

As with Hosea, however, the book exists not merely to condemn Israel, but to affirm Judah. It is from Jerusalem that Yahweh 'roars' and the book ends with a promise that the 'falling hut' of David (the temple) will be rebuilt. This must refer to the temple in Jerusalem that replaced Bethel in the late fifth century. So, we can determine when and why this book entered the scribal repertoire.

Obadiah

We know only the name 'Obadiah', which, like perhaps Joel and Malachi (below), may be an invented name for anonymous writing ('Obadiah' means 'servant of Yahweh'). Or it might, like Jonah, point to a prophet in the books of Kings (here 1 Kings 18, a contemporary of Elijah). The book deals with Edom, Judah's southern neighbour (and derived from Jacob's brother, Esau), which is criticized for betraying the fraternal bond and standing aside as others profited from Jacob's misfortune. The accusation makes sense after Edom's expansion into Judahite territory after the fall of the kingdom. The promise here is that the people of 'Israel' (meaning Judah) will regain lost lands not only from Edom, but also from the Philistines and from the Canaanites. The idea of a Judahite kingdom ruling over the lands of both provinces fits the ideology of both Kings and Chronicles, brought to reality by the Hasmonean kingdom of the second–first centuries BCE.

Jonah

The story of Jonah probably needs no introduction. This is not a book of oracles or visions but a parable about a prophet, based on the character in 2 Kings 14:25. Commissioned to call Nineveh to repentance, Jonah flees to the coast, taking a ship to Tarshish (Spain? Tarsus?). A storm brews and the sailors cast lots to see who has angered the god. Jonah is chosen and cast overboard (at his request), all but drowning when he is swallowed by a big fish (*not* a whale). In its belly he prays and is spewed out onto dry land. Then he heads for Nineveh, makes his announcement, and the city repents in grand style. Yahweh revokes the threat, so Jonah complains that he knew this would happen, and wanted the city destroyed! Yahweh rebukes him: he cares for all his creation.

Like many of Jesus's parables, the story is less simple than it appears. Never mind the fish: the exorbitant Assyrian repentance is the real miracle, and it contrasts with the reactions of Judah or Israel. But the real target of the book, however, is Jonah himself, a prophet who succeeds brilliantly, but wants to fail, and criticizes Yahweh for keeping his word! But

Yahweh does not wish to destroy other nations. Or does he? The reader may realize that, as with Sodom (Genesis 18–19), a divine promise to relent can always be revoked, and they would certainly be aware that Nineveh *had* been destroyed (in 612)!

Jonah's story is taken up in the New Testament. In Matthew 12 and Luke 11, Jesus is asked for a sign, giving in reply the 'sign of Jonah'. In Matthew, this sign is the three days and nights inside the fish. But in Luke, Jonah becomes a sign to the *Ninevites*: how, exactly, we are not told. Mark 4, Matthew 8 and Luke 8 tell a story of Jesus sleeping in the hull of a boat while a storm rages, a detail strikingly reminiscent of Jonah's behaviour. 'Something greater than Jonah is here' say Matthew 12:41 and Luke 11:32. Is Jonah's story even the basis for Jesus's three days (which are actually only two) in the tomb?

One more puzzle. 'Should I not be concerned', says Yahweh in the closing verse, 'about Nineveh, this huge city? There are more than 120,000 people in it who do not know their right hand from their left—and many animals, too.' A patronizing put-down for a great imperial capital? Or that Yahweh cares even for animals? An apparently simple story can provoke much thought.

Micah

Micah is presented as a contemporary of Isaiah from Judah, who prophesied to Samaria and Jerusalem. The book has three sections, each beginning with 'Listen!' and containing pronouncements of doom and hope (chapters 1-2; 3–5; 6–7). The doom awaits the rich and powerful, and prophets who will say whatever they are bribed to (3:5-7). Micah, of course, is not one of these: he has the prophetic spirit (3:8). While Judah and Samaria are threatened, Jerusalem ('Zion') is promised restoration. From Bethlehem (5:2-4) a king will come, hinting at another David. This is not lost on Matthew, who quotes it in his story of Jesus's birth (2:6). But Micah tells how this king will defeat the Assyrians. Could Hezekiah, a hero in Kings and Chronicles, have been in mind? But he lost to the Assyrians! And he was not born in Bethlehem. So, some other king—but in the near or the distant future?

Micah and Isaiah share the same historical setting and also a few verses, the best known being the turning of swords into ploughshares (Micah 4:1-4; Isaiah 2:1-4). And both contain predictions of deportation to Babylon and reflect the end of native monarchy. But Micah's future Davidic ruler and Isaiah's 'Servant' are quite different, as are their scenarios of future relationship with other nations, a matter on which the editors of the prophetic corpus clearly had divided opinions.

Nahum

Nahum's name, meaning 'comfort', is ironic, and given the lack of biographical details and several words and themes taken from other prophetic books, we may suspect an invented author. It deals, like Obadiah, with a single event and a single foreign enemy—the fall of Nineveh. Assyria had destroyed Israel, but this book is addressed to Judah, which became an Assyrian vassal from the mid-eighth century. Yahweh is here depicted as a mighty warrior who will ravage Nineveh for her guilt of bloodshed against many nations, and it is the Assyrian capital that is depicted as a harlot who will be publicly humiliated. The book ends with a dirge for the Assyrian king.

Habakkuk

Again, we have only the name of Habakkuk, and no details of this prophet or his time. The book is, unusually, in the form of a dialogue. It opens with a plea to Yahweh: 'how long must I put up with injustice?' The reply is: 'I am bringing on the Babylonians', with a description of their military forces. The prophet responds by saying he will wait to see what will happen, what God will say next. Again, Yahweh replies: 'Write down what I say: its message should be carried around and read out. It will reveal the future, but not necessarily right away'. The Babylonians, it turns out, will in the end suffer too.

The third chapter, headed 'a prayer of Habakkuk the prophet' seems to have been added later. It praises the power of the mighty divine warrior at whose march the earth trembles, and laments the present distress, while trusting in Yahweh's deliverance. At the very end is the kind of notation found in some Psalm headings, directing it to be sung to musical accompaniment—a hint of liturgical usage? Perhaps, but remember that silent reading was not the custom in those days, and an individual might also choose to chant.

Habakkuk's importance lies in its later use. The Dead Sea Scrolls include a commentary on the book, and 2:4, 'the righteous lives by his faith', is quoted both there and in Romans 1:17, Galatians 3:11 and Hebrews 10:38. In the New Testament, the 'faith' is directed to Jesus, but the book itself must refer to trust in God, specifically that, despite his apparent lack of intervention, he will indeed act in the future—at some point!

Zephaniah

In Zephaniah, the 'Day of Yahweh' described by Joel reappears. According to the superscription, the contents were delivered during the reign of Josiah (ca. 640–609), a generation before the end of the kingdom of Judah, which is vividly predicted as a divine sacrificial meal. From Judah, the prophet's gaze moves to the Philistines, those other major occupants of Palestine, whose fate will be the same as for the Ammonites and Moabites across the Jordan. But the scope keeps expanding: Ethiopia and Assyria will also fall to the divine warrior. In chapter 3, the topic reverts briefly to the sins of Jerusalem, but finally the terrifying Day of Yahweh turns into a day of joy. His people will be meek, truthful, and living peacefully. Yahweh will restore them and lead them.

Haggai and Zechariah

Haggai and Zechariah form a pair of characters: in Ezra 5 and 6 they are named together, and their books open with the same formula, dated by the reign of Persian kings. Both address themselves to the rebuilding of the temple in Jerusalem, placed at the end of the sixth century. But this dating may be calculated to fulfil the 70-year timescale prescribed in Jeremiah and elsewhere for the 'exile'. A more likely date of temple rebuilding is another 70 years later.

Haggai, unusually for a prophetic book, is in prose and consists of four separate pronouncements. The first (chapter 1) states that the people have not yet built a house for Yahweh and as a result are suffering drought. To this challenge the lay and religious leaders, Zerubbabel and Joshua, respond by beginning to construct a temple. The second (2:1-9) is an address from Yahweh to the builder: even though this is a poor structure compared to its predecessor, Yahweh will fill it with glory and treasure. The third (2:10-19) sees the prophet again prompted to reproach the people, this time for their ritual uncleanness, a reason for the drought they are suffering. The fourth section (2:20-23) prophesies that Yahweh will 'shake the heavens and the earth' and affirms that the governor Zerubbabel has indeed been divinely chosen.

Zechariah contains two different parts. Only the first belongs with Haggai and it starts (1:1-6) with a brief call to the people to 'turn to Yahweh', unlike their ancestors. The main section (1:7-6:15) consists of eight visions of the restoration of Jerusalem, which resemble the visions of Daniel in having angelic messengers who interpret. The visions are of a man on a red horse; of four horns; of a surveyor; and of Joshua the high priest standing beside Satan who is ready to accuse him; a menorah, the sacred candlestick; a flying scroll; an ephah (a measuring basket); and chariots. These visions (some of which have inspired Revelation) all relate to the restoration of the city and people, the divine blessing, and the overthrow of the nations. There is also a hint that Zerubbabel and Joshua are being designated as royal and priestly 'messiahs'. The hope of two messiahs is attested in a range of Jewish writings from the fifth century BCE onwards, and may even be hinted at in Luke's pairing of Jesus and John the Baptizer as being related, with John of a priestly family.

Chapters 9–14 are undated prophecies of an unnamed prophet. They envisage the destruction of not only the nation's enemies, but also its own leaders (like Isaiah 56–66). These chapters also foresee the regathering of the 'lost' tribes of Israel and the pouring out of the divine spirit (as in Joel). Zechariah has also been utilized in the gospels: 'they shall look on him whom they have pierced', in 12:10 (see John 19:37; also Revelation 1:7), and especially the call in 9:9 to Zion to rejoice: 'Your king is coming to you, true and victorious, humble and riding on a donkey', enacted in Jesus's entry into Jerusalem (Matthew 21; Mark 11, Luke 19; John 12).

Malachi

Malachi's name ('my messenger') may have been lifted from 3:1 (see below). Biographical data are lacking, and it is suspected that Malachi was invented to bring the total of minor prophets to twelve. Because the first word, 'oracle' (Hebrew *massa*), is also used in Zechariah 9 and 12, the contents of the book may have been detached from there.

Malachi contains six dialogues beginning with a rebuke from either God or the prophet. The themes are familiar: God has punished Edom (e.g. Obadiah), the priests are offering unworthy sacrifices (Ezekiel, Third Isaiah), the people are withholding their tithe offering, Judah has abandoned the laws of the covenant, and God's judgment will separate the righteous from the wicked on the 'day of Yahweh' (Joel, Amos). What is new here is the coming of 'my messenger' (Hebrew *malachi*) in 3:1 before Yahweh's judgment. That person, we learn from 4:5, is Elijah. This 'messenger' creates a strong link between the Testaments, with John the Baptizer as the announcer of Jesus, and as Elijah returned (e.g. Matthew 17; Luke 1:17). Thus, Mark's Gospel in particular reinforces that the gospel of Jesus begins as the Jewish scriptures finish.

DANIEL

The book of Daniel was not included within the Prophets in the Hebrew Bible, but in the Writings. This may be because it was completed and canonized after the prophetic collection, including the twelve Minor Prophets, was complete. Much of Daniel (chapters 2–7) is also in Aramaic. It can be described as an 'apocalyptic' book, though more accurately, its second part (chapters 7–12) contains apocalypses. The first six chapters are courtier tales, like Esther, the Joseph story (Genesis 39–50), and Tobit. In such tales the hero succeeds through cleverness, prudence, foresight and sometimes luck. The role of the deity is usually hidden, but not here: Daniel's ability to interpret dreams is due to God, and so is his deliverance from persecution.

The theme of the whole book is that world politics are ordained by the Jewish god, who appoints the rulers of four successive empires (Babylonian, Median, Persian and Greek) and frustrates attempts by them to challenge him. His plan for the course of world history can be revealed only by him. The kings receive dreams or visions that symbolize the future, and Daniel interprets these. Later, angels interpret their own visions. The culmination of all the visions (except chapter 5, about Belshazzar's feast) is a final kingdom that will not end. The events leading to that kingdom become more detailed towards the end of the book and correspond with what we know to have occurred (more or less) up to a certain point, when the outcome does not materialize as predicted. This point gives us the date of completion, which is confirmed by the book's increasing focus on the cessation of the temple sacrifice, a measure of the Seleucid (Syrian) king, Antiochus IV, which was successfully reversed in 164. The two stories of persecution in chapters 3 and 6 (the furnace and the lions' den) do not reflect Jewish experience in foreign lands, but rather allude to persecution in Judah at this time. Another indication of Daniel's second-century BCE date is its fleeting reference to resurrection in chapter 12. This doctrine, spelt out nowhere else in the Old Testament, had by now been accepted by the Pharisees, and is taken for granted in the New Testament.

Daniel's predictions were reinterpreted by readjusting the identity of the empires to designate Rome, not Greece, as the fourth kingdom. Christians did the same, while Jesus was identified with the 'son of man' (human figure: compare Ezekiel 1) enthroned in Daniel 7:13-14, who 'comes with the clouds of heaven' and is given an 'everlasting dominion that shall not pass away'.

Daniel is a diviner who reads signs, a mantic. Scriptural texts also began to function as signs, and in chapter 9 Daniel puzzles over Jeremiah's prediction of a 70-year exile before it is interpreted for him. The Dead Sea Scrolls also feature a 'Teacher' who had the gift of understanding the prophetic 'mysteries'. This process is precisely how the New Testament gospel appropriates the Jewish scriptures.

Chapter Twelve

Law, Wisdom and Prayer

BIBLICAL ETHICS

The Bible's moral teaching is actually not very remarkable. For the most part, it is typical of the values of the age in which the writers lived. It does not advocate democracy, freedom of speech or equality, whether sexual, racial, or religious. Women are subordinate, unbelievers are evil, slavery is acceptable. Its god is gracious to believers and vengeful to unbelievers, demanding obedience and even love. Like all gods, he expects sacrifice. The Bible is, with a very occasional lapse, monotheistic, and accepts that God is the source of all virtue. But the problem of evil is never definitively solved, either, and God cannot easily be acquitted of compliance.

Here, we explore three ways in which ethical as well as metaphysical issues are expressed and debated in the Bible. These are law, wisdom and prayer. The ethic of the New Testament operates under a new dispensation, that of the 'spirit', but Christian behaviour conforms very closely to conventional Jewish morality.

LAW

'Law' is not the ideal translation of the Hebrew *torah*, which means 'teaching'. Nor is 'commandment' or 'judgment' the best translation of *mishpat*. 'Custom' is much more preferable, and custom was the manner in which morality was set and enforced, while (priestly) teaching governed matters of cultic observance. In the ancient Near East, kings liked to assume responsibility for justice in their realm, and, like Hammurabi in his famous lawcode, to represent their laws as handed to them by the gods, or as exercised on behalf of the gods. In reality, while kings could represent a court of appeal, morality and justice were matters of local custom, locally adjudicated by elders. Laws of the generalized form 'you shall not...' represent general principles, but do not set out penalties, nor distinguish different kinds of slaughter. Laws of the form 'if someone does x', followed by a prescribed punishment, suggest a uniform system. Finally, *huq*, translated 'ordinance', hints at something engraved. But in Deuteronomy, for example, all terms denoting prescribed behaviour are treated as comprising the corpus of written Mosaic *torah*. Within Judaism, this law only gradually acquired a normative value and, at first, only among certain parties (Pharisees, scribes, authors of the Dead Sea Scrolls). Under the empires, legal administration was usually handled by assigning matters to ethnic groups who shared customs. Only issues between ethnic groups required negotiation or intervention. Within Christian communities, ethnic differences created problems, which is why so many of the letters have to prescribe basic rules.

The Deuteronomic covenant law in theory amounted to equating morality with obedience. But the theory mattered little as long as the divine law corresponded to custom with which the foreign ethnicities imported into Samaria after 722 needed to become acquainted (2 Kings 17 describes such a process). The one overriding morality of the covenant law was *hesed*, meaning 'loyalty' between patron and client. That the divine patron should behave disloyally is not contemplated, and in any case the client has no redress. The relationship (and thus Israel's religion as Deuteronomy sees it) is a matter of mutual interest.

But if Yahweh is the god of all, what relationship, and what conditions, apply to other nations? Think of Amos 9:7: "'Are you not like the Ethiopians to me, people of Israel?" says Yahweh. "Did I not bring Israel up from the land of Egypt, and the Philistines from Crete and the Arameans from Kir?"' The Old Testament does not expect that non-Israelites would or should obey the Mosaic law because that was Israel's special possession, making them unique. But international ethical conventions are implied in Amos and other prophets, and other covenants besides with Israel. In Genesis 9:17, God says to Noah, 'This is the sign of the covenant that I have established between me and all flesh that is on the earth', including not consuming the blood of animals. (Here is the basis of the apostolic ruling about non-Jews.) Accordingly, not only Genesis, but Hebrews and 2 Peter name Noah as 'righteous', in a fully Christian sense (defying the later Christian doctrine of universal human sinfulness since Adam).

Paul does not necessarily sever law from ethics, but regards 'sin' as too powerful for the law to overcome. 'Works' are not bad but without 'faith' they will save no-one. Within Judaism, however, 'law' was, with a

Figure 6: Hammurabi, the Babylonian king, receiving laws from the god Shamash

few zealous exceptions, never a matter of performing ordained tasks, nor is 'holiness' the same as 'righteousness'. Whether by rejecting 'law' Paul leaves an ethical vacuum is something for theologians to consider, though most don't.

WISDOM

The group of writings that the Christian Bible designated 'poetical books' contains mostly what scholars now call 'Wisdom'. Wisdom is both something external, a body of truth, and also the human quality of possessing such truth. It embraces metaphysics as well as ethics, and even combines them in addressing the nature of God, the world, and humanity's place in it. It is also not specifically an Israelite or Jewish enterprise, but is found all over the ancient Near East. Indeed, even in the scriptures it has a universal applicability.

There are four main genres of wisdom writing. One is instructional: practical advice for living a successful life, exemplified most clearly in Proverbs, Ecclesiastes and Sirach. Another is the extended discourse, probing metaphysical and existential issues, in the same three books but also in Job and the Wisdom of Solomon. A third is the 'wisdom tale' which illustrates how wisdom operates and how it brings success, such as Tobit. The genre of apocalypse is also sometimes described as 'mantic wisdom', and this hints at a fundamental tension within the Old Testament, especially between a wisdom that is learned and one that is revealed. That God is its source is not disputed, but rather how wisdom is learnt and gained.

'Wisdom', which we could more helpfully translate as 'philosophy', accepts the existence of gods as the explanation for the existence and meaning of the world. But since God created the world, the 'wise' of the Bible infer his nature and will from that created world, anticipating the medieval Christian 'natural theology' that anticipated the religion of the Enlightenment. The god of Wisdom is a creator, not a lawgiver nor a saviour, and he has no allegiance to any one nation. The oppositions within Wisdom are not between Israel and other nations but between 'wise' and 'foolish', 'righteous' and 'wicked', 'true' and 'false'. Nevertheless, efforts to harmonize Wisdom and Torah are apparent in some Psalms, in the Wisdom of Solomon and, in a Platonic or Stoic fashion, in Philo of Alexandria.

Wisdom is especially associated with the figure of Solomon; and Proverbs, Ecclesiastes and the Song of Solomon form a 'Solomonic' canon, being ascribed to the legendary 'wise' king. As explained in Chapter 2, attributing literary works to eminent authors is a feature of Old Testament canon formation (law with Moses, Psalms with David). The story in 1 Kings 4 of Solomon's request to be given 'wisdom' already hints at the idea that wisdom can be revealed as well as learnt.

Proverbs

Proverbs is not a single composition with a single author, but an anthology. In chapter 31 are 'the words of King Lemuel', in 30:1 'the words of Agur son of Jakeh' (both unknown), and then 'sayings of the wise' in 24:23. The collection contains one- or two-liners, short admonitions and some longer speeches. According to the introduction (1:2-6), the addressee is to learn and to discern, that is, use judgment, finding out what the 'sayings' and 'riddles' of the wise really mean. 'Fear of Yahweh', we are told more than once (1:7; 9:10), 'is the beginning of wisdom' ('respect' might be a better translation), and sinners should be avoided. But on the logic of Proverbs, 'sinning' and 'foolishness' are the same thing.

Wisdom and foolishness are both personified as female. Lady Wisdom cries out in the street, promising ease and security to those who listen, disaster to those who do not. Loose women lead the other way. To a young man (the implied reader), a choice between potential brides is a neat way to depict moral choices, as well as to convey the difficulty of the right choice. But there is more to the metaphorical conceit of 'Lady Wisdom'. She claims (3:19; 8:22-36) that she was with Yahweh when he created the world, as his assistant. She is, then, in a serious way, a disguised consort of Yahweh who, we know from inscriptions and from references in the Old Testament, was called Asherah. Philosophically, the role of Ms. Wisdom declares that the world was created in a way that is both logical and moral. Experience and observation can show this. For example, the busy ant (6:6) teaches the value of industry and the folly of laziness. Certain behaviours thus bring success, others failure. But these outcomes do not result from direct divine intervention. They are natural: this is the way the world works. And, it goes without saying, such a world does not need either perfecting or ending. It just needs more education.

Before acquiring experience, the addressee is urged to learn wisdom from parents, and many of the little speeches begin 'my child'. A lot of what passes for 'wisdom' seems like commonsense and there is a good deal of repetition. Keep away from evil people, avoid laziness, control your speech, respect God. Some of the virtues (hard work, for example) are those of the farmer, or artisan or trader. But several are pertinent especially to the elite: prudence, reticence and correct demeanour before kings.

Proverbs places God at the centre of a universe in which the metaphysical and the ethical coincide. But Wisdom does not end here, and other books take us beyond this simple thesis. For, after all, the world does *not* really look like this, except perhaps for a privileged few. Pressed between Job and Ecclesiastes, Proverbs is squeezed from both sides by doubt. (In the Hebrew canon this does not work: Proverbs follows Psalms, as Solomon follows David, while Job follows both.)

Job

The story of Job is a challenge to the philosophy of Proverbs. Its thesis is simple: a righteous man suffers. But the book consists of a prose framework around a set of poetic dialogues, and each part gives a different answer. According to the prose story, Job suffers because the Satan (who is Yahweh's own appointed 'Grand Inquisitor', acting only under orders) notices his exceptional goodness, but also because he notices the good life that Job has. The Satan asks, very reasonably, whether Job is merely good for the sake of his rewards, in which case he loves God only for gain. This is a challenge that Yahweh has to answer, and so he agrees to test Job's piety by allowing the Satan to take away his possessions (including children) and then to attack Job's body as well. His wife tempts him to curse God (as the Satan had predicted he would). But he does not. At the end of the story, Job has, in effect, vindicated God, and has everything restored to him, with interest. The lesson of the story seems to be that when the righteous suffer, they are being tested and should keep faith in God, awaiting their recompense. It's actually almost identical to the message of Daniel: if the present is bad, God will soon make it right. The Satanic charge of selfish piety, however, does not go away with this answer, and God is not really vindicated.

In the dialogues between Job and three friends, plus another called Eliphaz, our hero has no idea why he is afflicted and asks God many times to appear and explain. His friends assure him that he must have sinned and that God should not be challenged. There is much more to this beautiful poetry, but the outcome is that God confronts Job, and rebukes him for his ignorance and conceit: How dare you challenge me! My creation is too wonderful for you to comprehend. Job accepts this answer, which is perhaps the most convincing and bravest answer in the whole of the scriptures: humans cannot in the end understand God. Such an answer frees God from human demands of justice and leaves philosophy dumb.

But the prose and the poem together display God in a very bad light, because in the prose story, God tells Job that he was right to insist on his innocence, while God's rebuke of Job's ignorance is pretty hollow, since the prose introduction has made God's motivation very understandable indeed. How was this mess allowed?

One answer may be that a poem on the theme of human suffering as a mystery, denying divine justice, was intolerable, but rather than abandon it, a story was supplied to affirm it—even at the expense of making God look devious. Since the poetry does not refer to 'Yahweh' while the prose does, we can certainly suspect different authors. And we shall see presently that Ecclesiastes, which also denies divine justice, has likewise been glossed. Clumsy as the result may be, the belief in resurrection that was to dawn soon after these texts reached their present form suggests there was, in the end, no explanation of undeserved suffering within this life.

Some verses of Job have given rise to Christian interpretations of resurrection and of a Redeemer. For example, a modern translation of Job 19:25-27 runs:

> I know that my Redeemer lives,
> and that at the last he will stand upon the earth;
> and after my skin has been thus destroyed,
> then in my flesh I shall see God,
> whom I shall see on my side,
> and my eyes shall behold, and not another.

But the poetry of Job is often difficult (indeed, it is the most difficult Hebrew of the Hebrew Bible), and a literal translation would run as follows:

> I know that my advocate is alive
> and after he will stand on the dust,
> once my skin has been peeled off,
> and I will see God whom I see for myself
> and my eyes have seen and not a stranger...

It is quite possible that this passage contains some copying errors and perhaps other scribal interventions. One might argue, all the same, that the Christian gospel does constitute an explanation of the problem of apparently innocent suffering, the justice of God, and the hope of a final reward. But it is *an* explanation, and not necessarily *the* explanation. Indeed, such a thing may not even exist.

Ecclesiastes

'Ecclesiastes' (Hebrew *Qoheleth*) means one who performs in an assembly; a speaker, an orator. The philosopher declares that he has sought to find out for himself what humans can gain from their 'work' or 'toil' (perhaps their 'activity' in general). But since everyone, including himself, will perish like animals, it is hard to find any point or purpose. What everything 'under the sun' amounts to is 'vanity', or, better, 'futility'. Not only can humans not understand it: there is nothing to be understood. In an oft-quoted song in chapter 3, events have their seasons: a time to be born and die, to weep and laugh, keep and lose, love and hate, as if in an inevitable, meaningless cycle. Yet pleasure can be found, and when it is, it must be celebrated, for it will pass soon enough. Death awaits all, the righteous and unrighteous equally.

The Orator identifies himself as 'son of David, king in Jerusalem', which makes this pseudepigraphic, for there is no way it comes from the legendary king. But the Solomonic mask is perhaps significant. For what good did his wisdom do Solomon, since, according to Kings, he lost most of his kingdom? Is the answer that at least he took his pleasure (numerous wives, wealth) when he had the opportunity?

The sentiments of the Orator are obviously as troublesome as those of Job to the conventional theologies of the scriptures. So, we find the occasional comment that undermines this existentialist philosophy (e.g. 2:26). And in the closing verses we encounter these varied responses (12:10-14). First of all, in his defence:

> The Teacher sought to find pleasing words, and he wrote words of truth plainly. The sayings of the wise are like goads, and like nails firmly fixed are the collected sayings that are given by one shepherd.

But now comes a warning about going any further:

> Of anything beyond these, my child, beware. Of making many books there is no end, and much study is a weariness of the flesh.

And finally, putting matters straight:

> The end of the matter; all has been heard. Fear God, and keep his commandments; for that is the whole duty of everyone. For God will bring every deed into judgment, including every secret thing, whether good or evil.

We can see from carefully comparing the Old Testament books that behind them lie debates and disputes. But it is not often that these appear in such a clear manner.

The Song of Songs (or Song of Solomon)

Despite the heading 'The Song of Songs, which is Solomon's', this collection of love poetry does not necessarily claim Solomonic authorship, because a female voice also speaks in the poem, and Solomon is featured as a character. It is not Wisdom, but rather love, between a king and a dark-skinned 'Shulammite' (1:5-7 may be a feminized equivalent of Solomon, like Papageno and Papagena in Mozart's opera *The Magic Flute*).

These erotic poems share interlinked themes and images, and are exchanged between two (probably unmarried) lovers, in an idyllic setting but with at least one scene in a city (Jerusalem?). But what explains their inclusion in the scriptures? Jewish and Christian interpreters have provided their own answer: that the love-affair was an allegory of the love of God for Israel or of Jesus for the Church or for the soul of the believer. But the history of interpretation does not necessarily provide the historical answer. There are some works of a secular or at least not overtly theological character, like Esther and Ruth, deemed worthy of inclusion in the Jewish literary canon. If the Song suggests no plausible pretext for its inclusion, then let us accept that, as with Ecclesiastes, the scribes liked the idea of provocation.

Wisdom (or the Wisdom of Solomon)

This apocryphal book, originally written in Greek, is an eloquent praise of Wisdom, addressed at first to earthly rulers. Its opening address (1–5) may well include a rebuttal of Ecclesiastes (see 2:1-9), and it turns into a condemnation of the ungodly, dwelling on their ultimate fate. Parts of it have a place in Catholic liturgy, though it is virtually ignored by Protestants. Unlike the other books of philosophy, it expresses a belief in immortality and thus the idea of the soul as separate from the body. This was a general assumption in the Greek-speaking world, and it allows good and evil to be recompensed in the other world without the need for a bodily resurrection. Let us not wonder about the consequence of Jesus having an immortal soul! But at least the Wisdom of Solomon retains the idea of a 'day of judgment' (3:18). Also expressed is the belief that God did not intend death for humanity but that it was brought about by 'the devil's envy' (2:24).

A second section (6–9) also opens with a challenge to rulers and reads as if spoken by Solomon himself. Much of it is a praise of Wisdom, again in the image of a woman who is God's constant companion. A humble prayer to God, modelled on Solomon's prayer in 1 Kings 3:6-9, concludes this. The final section (10–19) celebrates Wisdom's work in history, from Adam to Joshua, acting as God's surrogate throughout. This becomes a passage of praise addressed to God himself in guiding Israel, where the worship of gods 'made with human hands' is treated as Israel's great evil, leading to all manner of corruption. But now it is God rather than Wisdom who is Israel's guide. The book ends optimistically: 'For in everything, O Lord, you have exalted and glorified your people, and you have not neglected to help them at all times and in all places'. The likely place of composition is among the Greek-speaking Jewish diaspora, most likely Alexandria, and it represents a good example of how Jewish and Greek thought-worlds could mingle harmoniously.

Ben Sira (or Sirach, Ecclesiasticus)

This book claims to be a (Greek) translation of the writings of Jesus (Yeshua) ben Sira, by his grandson, in Egypt in 132 BCE. A text of most of the Hebrew original was discovered in Egypt in 1897 and some fragments were more recently found at Qumran and in the fortress of Masada, near the Dead Sea. It is, like Proverbs, a mixture of practical proverbs and longer discourses. As in the Wisdom of Solomon, we find a rehearsal of Israel's history through a list of great figures from Abraham to Nehemiah to the contemporary high priest Simeon. The personification of Wisdom as a woman also recurs. Traditional Jewish ideas are flavoured rather than mixed with Greek ideas, for ben Sira was quite a traditionalist, living in Jerusalem and venerating its cult and priesthood. He does not believe in a resurrection or an immortal soul, and whereas *Wisdom* blames death on the devil, ben Sira blames it on women, and Eve in particular. The practical ethics here are also typically biblical: care for the poor, justice, respect for God's law. A nice example of ben Sira's blend of the practical and pious falls in chapter 38, concerning physicians. Respect the skill of the doctor, he says, for the Lord has given it, just as the Lord has created medicines. But before consulting a physician, purge yourself of sin and offer a sacrifice!

Like Wisdom, ben Sira creates within the Christian Bible a line of transition between the thought-worlds of the Hebrew Bible and the New Testament, from the world of western Asia to that of the Eastern Mediterranean. This cohesion is lost with the omission of the apocryphal books from many bibles and their relative neglect from the teaching of the Bible in schools and universities. For while Prophecy has become the major link between the Testaments in the Christian ordering and reading of scripture, Wisdom provides a more organic connection with the ethical teaching of the gospels and letters. In the elevation of the figure of Jesus's mother, Mary, in Catholic Christianity, we see, too, a startlingly exact image of the heavenly personified Wisdom of the Old Testament.

PRAYER (PSALMS)

Private piety increasingly characterized Judaism as it developed towards its classical formulation after the first century ce. This has been observed in the development of both Law and Wisdom as absorbed in the lifestyle of pious individuals and societies. Prayer is another major vehicle of personal devotion, and while prayers can be found throughout the Old and New Testaments, the book of Psalms is the preeminent collection.

The book of Psalms exhibits a wide variety of literary forms, and its opening recommends the wise to study Torah in order to flourish, perhaps pointing to the collection as an overwhelmingly private rather than public resource. We do not know, at any rate, either who wrote the Psalms or for what purpose. The belief that they were written by David developed gradually. He is mentioned in 73 of the headings, though whether the usual ascription should be translated 'by David' or 'for David' is unclear. But twelve psalms are ascribed to Asaph and eleven to the Korahites, while Psalms 72 and 127 are credited to Solomon. Still, 1 Chronicles 23–29 describes how David organized the entire temple cult, and his musicianship managed to calm Saul's 'evil spirit' by his playing of the lyre, according to 1 Samuel 16. By the time the Dead Sea Scrolls were written, David's fame as a composer of songs had mushroomed, as one of the Psalm scrolls testifies:

> ...and he wrote 3,600 psalms and songs to sing before the altar over the daily offering for all the days of the year, 364, and for the Sabbath offering 52, and for the offering of each new month and for festivals and the Day of Atonement, 30 songs...

The superscriptions also demonstrate efforts to connect some Psalms with events in David's life: Psalm 3 'when he fled from his son Absalom', Psalm 34 'when he pretended to be insane before Abimelech', or Psalm 52 'when Doeg the Edomite went and informed Saul'. Nevertheless, most Psalm headings (there are 116) specify the tune, or the musical accompaniment, or their intended recipient—'for the director' or even 'for the wise'. This prompts the question: what were the Psalms used for? An earlier scholarly theory was that they were part of the regular temple liturgy, its 'hymn-book'. But then we might have expected a more orderly arrangement to have developed. There is also little evidence of public hymn-singing in the temple, though according to the Chronicler, the Levites were accomplished choristers. But many psalms allude to individual circumstances, and so may have been available for private use when requesting divine relief from illness or other misfortune.

A few psalms do imply a public, ceremonial function, such as a group of pilgrim psalms (called 'Songs of Ascent', nos. 120–134), and a number of royal psalms, glorifying the king. One is Psalm 110: 'Yahweh says to my lord, "Sit at my right hand until I make your enemies your footstool"'. The possibility of some monarchic-era liturgies cannot be ruled out, of course, though in cultic performance God would later have to replace the human king. In Christianity (and in the Dead Sea Scrolls), the Psalms have also been read as prophetic. The verse from Psalm 110 quoted earlier is cited three times in the New Testament (Luke 20:43; Acts 7:49; Hebrews 1:13) and is interpreted in a prophetic sense, while Psalm 34:20 is cited in John 19:36 in describing the crucifixion ('none of his bones shall be broken').

Despite the many uncertainties about the origin of psalms, their use, and the development of the canonical collection, which the Dead Sea Psalms manuscripts show to have been fluid as late as the time of Jesus, the Psalms offer us some glimpses into the private piety of not just the scribal elite but probably many ordinary Yahweh worshippers. It is here more than anywhere else that the emotional power of religious belief radiates. The New Testament offers no comparable illustration.

Postscript

Two fashionable dimensions of biblical scholarship are reception and what is called vernacular or contextual reading. The first, accepting that the meaning of any text depends on the reader as well as the author and the text itself, explores how the meanings of the Bible have shifted with different political and social circumstances. Examples of major changes are the Protestant readings that followed the printing of the scriptures in vernacular languages and the political upheavals that ushered in the modern period, especially the Enlightenment. The Bible became a political tract, bringing into being the colonization of North America and the political complexion of the United States of America. More recently, feminism fomented a revolution that led to all kinds of readings against patriarchy, racism, sexual discrimination and all kinds of cultural hierarchy. These movements might well be seen as part of a growing secularism with regard to religious scriptures and religion itself, whereby biblical values are judged by contemporary social ones rather than the other way round.

Contextual or vernacular readings are a theological enterprise, their philosophical basis being that no one exegetical agenda can claim priority over any other. This is not unproblematic, either logically or politically, because some agendas are incapable of the kind of negotiation that rescues a contextual reading from solipsism. Fundamentalism is an example of such an agenda. But theologically and pragmatically, the belief that the Bible meets readers in different places and in different cultures, generating different meanings that are locally rather than universally valid, is helpful in a multicultural world. It even resonates with postmodern values that deconstruct normativities and regularities.

The realization that the Bible is not a wall of graffiti but a mirror, and that it responds to intelligent and open questions with intelligent and open answers, is the only guarantee of its future as a factor in the Western civilization that it helped to build. The purpose of this book has been to encourage readers to confront it in just this way.

Index

Aaron 21, 38
Abraham 3, 11, 36, 37, 38, 48, 81
Achan 41, 95, 123
Acts of the Apostles 33, 74, 75, 83, 85,
    90–91, 94–103
        authorship 90
        letters of Paul and 33, 94, 105, 106,
            110, 111
        prophecy 124, 134
Adad-nirari III 61
Adam 37, 78
Ahab 58, 61, 62
Ai 40–1, 55
Akhenaton 20
Alexandria 69, 72, 151
Ammon/Ammonites 37, 51, 138
Amos 126, 134–5, 139, 143
Ananias 95
angels 21, 87, 89, 96, 97, 107
        Daniel and 126, 138, 140
        rebel angels 78, 80, 115
        in Revelation 118, 119
Antioch 69, 97, 99, 100
Antiochus III 70
Antiochus IV 140
Antipater 72
apocalypses 80–1, 117, 123, 126, 140, 145
Apocrypha 9, 34, 131, 150, 151–52
    see also semi-canonical books
Apollos 99, 109, 110
apostolic tradition 12–13
archaeology 53–65
        beginnings of monarchy 57–60
        history and 53–56

Israelite kingdom 61
Israelite settlement 56
Jerusalem 58
Judah 61–65
periodization 54–55
Aristobulus 72
Artaxerxes 46, 47
Assyria/Assyrians 28, 30, 35, 36, 44–45, ·
    125
Athaliah 62

Babylonia/Babylonians 28, 30, 35, 46,
    129–30
baptism
        as conversion rite 98, 110
        of Jesus 86, 115
        Paul on 110
Barnabas 85, 97
Baruch 129, 131
Benjamin 36–7, 65
Benjamin, tribe of 41, 43, 44, 45, 46, 48,
    58, 60, 65, 111
Bethel 43, 65, 134, 135
biblical scholarship 5–6, 17–18, 20, 127,
    154
Book of the Twelve 16, 133
books of hours 11

Caesarea 72, 96, 100–1, 111
calendar 77–78, 81
Calvin, John 11
Canaan 37, 38, 40–41, 55
Catholic Epistles 115–16
Christian scripture 7, 9, 13–14

Chronicles 21, 34, 44–45, 46, 47, 58, 135, 152
circumcision 70, 96, 97, 108, 113
Colossians 85, 90, 112, 113
contextual reading 154
Corinth 99, 100
Corinthians 108, 109–10, 113, 125
Cornelius 96
council of Jerusalem 97, 108
creating a Bible 6–10
Crispus 95
Cyrus, King of Persia 45, 127

Daniel 30, 48, 106, 138, 140–41, 147
    calendars 81
    Revelation and 117–20, 123, 126
    'son of man' 82, 88, 89
David 11, 13, 41–42, 45, 125
    chronology 57–58
    'house of David' 16, 22, 44, 62, 64
    Jerusalem and 42
    Jesus as 'son of David' 86, 88, 89
    psalms and 16, 152–53
Day of Atonement 39, 47, 78, 114, 152
deacons 12, 95–96, 113
Dead Sea Scrolls 10, 15, 24, 77, 114, 152
    Jeremiah 129
    the Messiah 82
    Psalms 153
    the Teacher 141
Deuteronomy 21, 23, 34, 38, 39–40, 130
    covenant law 124, 143
    Deuteronomic theology 123–24
Deutero-Pauline letters 112–14
divination 123
    see also prophecy
dualistic beliefs 80, 116, 120

Ecclesiastes 6, 10, 19, 147, 148, 149–50
Egypt 17, 30, 37, 50–51, 53–54, 58
Elijah 30, 43, 87, 139
Elisha 30, 43
Elohim 20, 35
Enoch 24, 77, 78, 80–81, 115, 119, 123, 126

Enuma Elish 35
Ephesians 112, 113–14
Ephesus 99, 100, 109, 111, 112
Esau 37, 135
Esdras 47
Essenes 77
Esther 10, 30, 48, 140, 150
Exodus 34, 38, 72, 90
Ezekiel 21, 88, 126, 127, 129, 131–32, 139, 140
    Revelation and 117–20, 123
Ezra 34, 46–8, 64, 77, 131, 138

Finkelstein, Israel 55, 57
Flood, the 35, 78, 107
foreigners 47, 48–49

Galatians 96, 97, 108–9, 110, 137
Gamaliel 95
Garden of Eden 35, 78, 119, 120
Gedaliah 44, 129, 130
genealogies 35–37, 44
    Jesus 37, 40, 91
Genesis 16, 19, 34–37, 93, 114, 120, 136, 140
    Abraham and Isaac 11
    calendar 78–9
    Enoch 81
    Jacob 34, 36, 60, 65
    Noah 97, 143
    Tower of Babel 95
Gilgamesh Epic 35
Gospels 6, 12, 13, 32
    as history 32–33
    Synoptic Gospels 84–91, 92, 93
    see also John; Luke; Mark; Matthew
Greek philosophy 75

Habakkuk 137
Haggai 138
Hammurabi 142
Hasmonean kingdom 70–72, 81, 82, 83, 135
Hebrew Bible 9, 10, 14, 140, 148, 151

Hebrews 7, 11, 40, 83, 104, 114–15, 137, 143, 153
Hellenism 69, 70
Herod Agrippa 72, 74, 97, 101
Herod the Great 51, 70, 74, 90, 97
Herodotus 28–29, 30, 36
Hezekiah 43, 44, 62, 127, 128, 136
history
    ancient historians 28–29
    the Gospels 32–33
    the 'historical Jesus' 32–33
    New Testament as 31–33
    Old Testament as 27–28, 29–31
Hosea 133, 134, 135

Isaac 11, 37, 91
Isaiah 16, 62, 86, 103, 123, 126, 127–29, 130, 131, 136, 139
    divine images 128
    messianic predictions 128–29
    Servant Songs 128
Israel 13–14, 28
    alternative history of 44–45
    archaeology 53–64
    becoming a nation 37–38
    defined by its law 38–40
    Judah as 46–48
    Judaism and 23–24
    kingdom of 61
    monarchy 41–44, 57–60
    the name 60
    national conception of 22–23
    occupying Canaan 40–41
    post-deportation gap 45–46
    prehistory of 34–37
    the 'Return' 64–65

Jacob 34, 36, 60, 65
James 87, 97, 100, 101
    epistle of 7, 13, 40, 115, 116
Jefferson, Thomas 7
Jehoram 62
Jehu 43, 61

Jeremiah 10, 64, 126, 127, 129–30, 138, 140–41
    Letter of 131
Jericho 40–1, 55
Jeroboam 43, 64
Jerome 9–10
Jerusalem 13, 45, 56, 70, 72
    in Acts 94, 95, 116
    archaeology 58
    council of Jerusalem 97, 108
    David and 42
    destruction 89, 127, 129, 131
    in Isaiah 127–28
    Jesus and 88, 89, 91, 92, 94, 139
    Paul and 96, 100
    restoration 22, 46, 47, 64, 130, 134, 138
    the 'Return' 64–65
Jerusalem temple 20, 70, 75, 132, 135
    building of 42, 45
    Ezekiel and 132
    Isaiah and 127, 129
    Jesus' cleansing of 88
    Psalms and 20, 152, 153
    rebuilding of 46, 47, 64, 72, 138
Jesus 9, 13, 14, 31, 69, 80, 129
    ascension 88, 91
    baptism 86, 115
    birth 6, 74, 90
    cleansing of the temple 88
    crucifixion and death 78, 86, 87, 92, 95, 115
    disciples 74–75
    divinity 6, 116
    genealogy 37, 40, 91
    in the Gospels 83–93
    the historical Jesus 32–33, 84
    Jerusalem and 88, 89, 91, 92, 94, 139
    Last Supper 92, 130
    as 'Messiah' 82, 86, 87
    ministry 86–87, 92
    miracles 87, 92
    Old Testament and 11, 15, 83–84

parables 5, 86–87, 91
resurrection 89, 90, 91, 98, 109–10
return 106–7, 112
titles 86, 87, 88, 89, 90, 93, 106–7,
    132, 140
transfiguration 115
trial 101
as Word 93
Jesus (Yeshua) ben Sira 151–52
Jewishness 13–14
Jewish scriptures 9, 13–14, 15, 83–84, 86,
    106, 114, 141
Joab 42, 125
Job 19, 145, 147–48
Joel 95, 124, 133–34, 138, 139
John the Baptist/Baptizer 80, 86, 87, 99,
    110, 128, 139
John, Gospel of 13, 14, 32, 64, 92–93, 108,
    116, 153
John, letters of 13, 116
Jonah 11, 101, 135–36
Joseph 36–7, 65, 140
Josephus 29–30, 70, 74
Joshua 23, 40–41, 95, 123, 138–39
Josiah 43, 47, 129, 138
Jubilees 77, 81
Judah 22–23, 40–46, 51, 56, 129, 130
    archaeology 57, 61–65
    as Israel 46–48
    provinces of 64–65
    records 28
Judaism 13
    ancient Judaisms 69–82
    apocalyptic books 80–81
    belief and practices 75–76, 96, 97
    forcible conversion 70
    Hebrew Bible 9, 10, 14
    the Messiah 82
    private piety 152
    rabbinic Judaism 81–82
    religions of 'Israel' and 23–24
Judaizers 76, 108
Judas Iscariot 74–75, 95
Jude 7, 13, 115, 116

Judges 23, 40, 41, 55, 62

Kings 23, 28, 41, 43, 44, 45–46, 64, 91, 123,
    127, 149
    1 Kings 18, 58, 87, 135, 146, 151
    2 Kings 62, 126, 127, 135, 143

Lamentations 10, 131
Law 10–11, 16, 34, 53, 142–45
letters of Paul 6, 7, 12, 33, 85, 96, 104,
    105–14
    Acts and 33, 94, 105, 106, 110, 111
    authentic letters 105–12
    Corinthians 108, 109–10, 113, 125
    Deutero-Pauline letters 112–14
    dissemination 111
    Ephesians 112, 113–14
    Galatians 96, 97, 108–9, 110, 137
    to Philemon 85, 90, 112
    Philippians 111
    Romans 110–11
    Thessalonians 106–8
    see also New Testament letters
Leviticus 11, 23, 38, 39, 78, 114
literacy 3, 17, 28, 31
literati 17, 19, 20, 21, 23, 30
    see also scribes
Luke, Gospel of 7, 13, 32–33, 37, 74, 75,
    83, 84–85, 89, 90–91, 100, 101, 128, 129,
    136, 139, 153
Luther, Martin 7, 9, 116

Maccabees 34, 49
Malachi 86, 135, 139
Marcion 7
Mark, Gospel of 13, 31, 32, 84, 85–89, 90,
    91, 128, 136, 139
Mary of Magdala 89, 92
Mary, mother of Jesus 11, 37, 89, 90, 91,
    152
Masoretic Text 9
Matthew, Gospel of 13, 32–33, 37, 40, 64,
    72, 84–85, 89–90, 107, 123, 128, 133,
    136, 139

Mazar, Amihai 57
Melchizedek 82, 106, 114
Merneptah 60
Mesha 62
Mesopotamia 17, 35, 36, 37, 123
Messiah, the 82, 86
    Jesus as 82, 86, 87
Micah 136
Moab 18, 37, 38, 48, 62
monarchy 41–44, 57–60
Moses 16, 37–38, 39, 72, 87
    books of 16, 34, 37–38
    Jesus and 90

Nahum 137
Napoleon Bonaparte 53–54
Nebuchadnezzar 44, 56, 64
Nehemiah 34, 46–48, 64, 77, 131
New Testament 12–13, 14
    Acts 33
    composition of 31
    dating 31
    as history 31–33
    prophecy in 124–5
    see also Acts of the Apostles;
        Gospels; New Testament letters;
        Revelation
New Testament letters 12, 104–16
    Catholic Epistles 115–16
    Colossians 112, 113
    Deutero-Pauline letters 112–14
    Ephesians 113–14
    Hebrews 40, 104, 114–15, 143
    James 116
    John 116
    Jude 116
    pastoral letters 112–13
    Pauline *see* letters of Paul
    Peter 115
    to Timothy 112–13, 114
    to Titus 112–13
Noah 6, 36–7, 107, 143
    covenant of Noah 97
Numbers 11, 34, 36, 38, 39

Obadiah 135, 137, 139
Old Testament 7–12, 14
    archaeology 53–64
    arrangement of books 9–10
    calendar 77–78
    collections and attributed authors
        15–17
    dating of 21–22
    divisions 10
    foreigners 48–49
    geography 50–51
    History 10, 11, 34, 48
    as history 27–28, 29–31
    Jesus and 11, 15, 83–84
    Law 10–11, 16, 34, 53, 142–45
    Moses story 16
    philosophy 19
    piety 19–20
    Poetry/Wisdom 10, 16
    politics 17–18
    priests 5–6, 20, 21, 38, 39, 40
    Prophecy 10, 11
    Psalms 5, 11, 16
    reasons for writing 20–21
    scribes 16, 17, 18
    scrolls 16
Omri, house of 60, 61, 62
Onesimus 112
oral literature 17, 28, 30
origin of sin 78

Papias, Bishop of Hierapolis 13, 85
Paul 10, 13, 32, 75, 78, 83, 90, 93
    in Acts 94, 96, 97–102
    on baptism 110
    chronology 103
    journeys 97–102
    on law 143, 145
    letters *see* letters of Paul
    Peter and 108–9
    on prophecy 124–25
    in Rome 102, 103
    speeches 103
    on women 109

Pentecost 95, 134
Peter 87
    in Acts 94, 96
    letters of 13, 85, 143
    Paul and 108–9
Pharisees 24, 70, 73–74, 86, 87, 90, 91, 95, 140, 143
Philemon 85, 90, 112
Philippians 111
Philistines 37, 42, 50–51, 58, 134, 138
Philo of Alexandria 75, 93, 145
philosophy 16, 19, 75, 145, 149
    see also wisdom writing
piety 19–20, 152
Pilate 89, 90
politics 17–18, 69–72
Polybius 29
Pompey 70, 72
priests 5–6, 20, 21, 38, 39, 40
prophecy
    New Testament 124–25
    Old Testament 10, 11
    Paul on 124–25
prophetic books 10, 11, 125–26
    Amos 126, 134–35, 139, 143
    Baruch 129, 131
    composition of 127
    Daniel *see* Daniel
    Ezekiel *see* Ezekiel
    Habakkuk 137
    Haggai 138
    Hosea 133, 134, 135
    Isaiah *see* Isaiah
    Jeremiah 10, 64, 126, 127, 129–30, 131, 138, 140–41
    Joel 95, 124, 133–34, 138, 139
    Jonah 135–36
    Lamentations 10, 131
    Letter of Jeremiah 131
    Malachi 86, 135, 139
    Micah 136
    minor prophets 133–39
    Nahum 137
    Obadiah 135, 137, 139

Zechariah 88, 117, 118, 126, 138–39
    Zephaniah 138
Proverbs 16, 93, 146–47
Psalms 5, 11, 16, 20, 95, 145, 152–53
    ceremonial function 153
    David and 16, 152–53
    as prophetic 153
Psalms of Solomon 82

Q (*Quelle*) 89, 91
Qur'an 3, 5

Rachel 36, 65
Rahab 40, 41, 48
Rapture, the 107
reception history of the bible 154
Rehoboam 43, 44, 58, 64
Revelation 7, 85, 92, 115
    Daniel and 117–20, 123, 126
Romans 110–11
Ruth 10, 30, 37, 48, 150

Sabbath, the 10–11, 35, 78
Sadducees 24, 70, 73–74, 86, 91
Samaria 22–23, 40, 45, 61, 70, 96, 129, 143
    provinces of 64–65
Samuel 23, 34, 41–42, 57, 58
    1 Samuel 48, 56, 91, 123, 126, 152
    2 Samuel 42, 125
Sargon of Agade 37, 38
Sargon II 61
Satan 78, 108, 119, 139, 147
Saul 30, 41–42, 48, 123, 152
scholarship 5–6, 17–18, 20, 127, 154
scribes 16, 17, 18, 86, 87, 90, 143
    see also literati
semi-canonical books 7, 9
    see also Apocrypha
Servant Songs 128
Shalmaneser III 61
Sheshonq 58
Simon the Zealot 74–75
sin, origin of 78
Sirach *see* Ben Sira

slaves/slavery 37, 40, 112, 142
Solomon 16, 42–43, 58, 146
 Psalms of Solomon 82
 wisdom writing 145–46, 150–51
Song of Songs/Song of Solomon 10, 16,
 145–46, 150
speaking in tongues 95, 109, 124
Stephen 96

Tamar 37, 42
Ten Commandments 11, 128
Thessalonians 106–8
Thomas 92
Thomas, Gospel of 33
Thucydides 29, 30
Timothy 97, 105, 109, 111, 112, 114
 2 Timothy 7, 85, 90, 113
Titus 112, 113
Tower of Babel 95

vernacular reading 154

wisdom writing 145–52
 Ben Sira 151–52
 Ecclesiastes 6, 10, 19, 145, 147, 148,
  149–50
 Job 145, 147–48
 mantic wisdom 145
 Proverbs 16, 93, 145, 146–47
 Song of Songs/Song of Solomon 10,
  16, 145–46, 150
 Wisdom/Wisdom of Solomon 145,
  150–51
women 40, 48, 91, 109, 142, 151

Zealots 74–75
Zechariah 88, 117, 118, 126, 138–39
Zephaniah 138
Zerubbabel 47, 138, 139

Lightning Source UK Ltd.
Milton Keynes UK
UKHW020307231118
332749UK00002B/32/P